EBENEZER STONES

EBENEZER STONES

USING AN ORDINARY STONE TO REMIND YOU
OF OUR EXTRAORDINARY GOD

CATHERINE MCDAUGALE

WALK BY FAITH
MEDIA, LLC
WALKBYFAITHMEDIA.COM

For Jesus
My Lord, my King, and my God.
May Your name be glorified!

Then Samuel took a stone and set it up between Mizpah and Shen, and called its name Ebenezer, saying, "Thus far the LORD has helped us."

— 1 SAMUEL 7:12

CONTENTS

INTRODUCTION

LET'S BE REAL. IT'S EASY TO GET OUR FOCUS OFF GOD. EVEN if we remember to seek Him first thing in the morning, we often get caught up in the tasks that need to be done as we go through the day. If you work in an office, you likely have to contend with emails, phone calls, and deadlines. Or if you work in a service-oriented job, you have to deal with people all day long. And moms who work in the home may feel frazzled by the seemingly never-ending laundry, cleanup, and disputes that arise throughout the day.

To make it worse, in the midst of the busyness, some of us tend to focus on the things that are wrong in our lives. Those negative thoughts seem to invite themselves in. Before you know it, your mind is consumed by something someone said or did, an incident at work, a wayward child, a husband who seems absent, or some other problem. You may even momentarily spiral down into despair.

Throughout my life, I have struggled with small bouts of depression. During those times, thoughts of past hurts or regrets seemed to run amok through my mind on instant replay. Entertaining those thoughts did nothing for me but keep me stuck. Immobile. Unable to take the next step.

The things you allow yourself to think about matter. Your thought life affects how you feel. It impacts your attitude and your decisions. Negative thoughts can alter the direction of your life, draining you of the courage to try something new or pursue a goal. Those thoughts can rob you of the joy that comes from paying attention to the beautiful things that are currently in your life.

And, yes, it's a choice. You can let your mind ponder those negative thoughts or you can redirect your thinking. You have control over what you think about.

A few years ago, God impressed on me the truth about His faithfulness. God has always been faithful in my life—despite the things I went through, the things I did, or the things I failed to do. And the truth is that God will always be faithful.

The Bible instructs us to meditate on "whatever things are true" (Philippians 4:8). Biblical meditation is different from the meditation that is practiced in yoga or other disciplines, in which you seek to empty your mind. The Greek word for meditate in Philippians means to reason or think on.[1] The New Living Translation tells us to "[f]ix your thoughts on." The idea is to ruminate or "chew on" those things.

So, to meditate on the truth of God's faithfulness, you will intentionally think about how God has been faithful. You will spend time remembering the things God has done.

As God taught me about His faithfulness, He showed me the ways that He has been faithful in my life. His loving hand has always been there—guiding, redirecting, protecting, helping, and providing. I can decide to meditate on the truth of

God's faithfulness. Or I can continue to let the thoughts about the negative things in my past or present flow through my mind.

When I purposefully think about God's faithfulness, my countenance is lifted. The things God has done and the way He does them is always so amazing. When I remember those things, a feeling of joy springs up from within me.

This book was born out of the work that God did in my life. God is not just faithful in my life, He is faithful in your life as well. God is faithful even when we are faithless because "He cannot deny Himself" (2 Timothy 2:13).

It doesn't matter what you've done. Regardless of your circumstances, the fact that God is faithful remains true. God does not change based on what happens in your life on a particular day. God remains the same. And He is faithful.

If you don't know much about God, this book will teach you about the fundamental ways that God is faithful in your life. And, if you've been walking with God for a while, you will be reminded about God's faithfulness. Either way, as we go on this journey, you will be able to see how God has been faithful in your life.

So grab your Bible and a cup of your favorite coffee or tea, and let's begin this journey together.

1

REMEMBERING GOD'S
FAITHFULNESS

WHAT IS AN EBENEZER STONE? IT'S A PHYSICAL REMINDER OF
something God has done in your life. The idea of using a
stone to help you remember God's faithfulness comes from the
Bible.

In 1 Samuel 7:12, it tells us about a time when "Samuel
took a stone and set it up between Mizpah and Shen, and
called its name Ebenezer, saying, 'Thus far the LORD has
helped us.'" Ebenezer is English for the Hebrew phrase "Eben
ha Ezer," which means "stone of the help."[1] Samuel set up the
stone as a memorial so everyone would remember where God
helped Israel to defeat the Philistines.

Samuel was not the first one to set up a stone of remembrance. In obedience to God's command, Joshua directed the
Israelites to set up stones by the Jordan River. He did so after
God had cut off the waters of the Jordan so they could pass
over into the land of Canaan on dry ground.

This was no small thing. God had made "the waters which
came down from upstream [stand] still, and [rise] in a heap

very far away" (Joshua 3:16). After the stones were set up, Joshua told the children of Israel,

> When your children ask their fathers in time to come, saying, "What are these stones?" then you shall let your children know, saying, "Israel crossed over this Jordan on dry land"; for the LORD your God dried up the waters of the Jordan before you until you had crossed over, as the LORD your God did to the Red Sea, which He dried up before us until we had crossed over, that all the peoples of the earth may know the hand of the LORD, that it is mighty, that you may fear the LORD your God forever. (Joshua 4:21-24)

Setting up the stones reminded Joshua's generation, and the generations who came after them, that God is powerful and strong. When we remember and meditate on the amazing things that God has done, we can't help but be in awe of Him. Doing so puts our minds in a right perspective—in which we give God the honor and respect He deserves, knowing that we cannot do the things He does.

The account also reminds us that God is our help. He is the One we should turn to in every circumstance. Jesus said, "Come to Me, all you who labor and are heavy laden, and I will give you rest" (Matthew 11:28). God wants us to rely on Him for our needs.

And it is evidence of God's faithfulness. God's faithfulness is great, and His mercies are new every morning (Lamentations 3:22-23). The Hebrew word for faithfulness or faithful is emunah (pronounced em-oo-naw), which means stability or steadfastness.[2] The word gives us a picture of security. God is stable and steadfast. He doesn't change. He is the "same yesterday, today, and forever" (Hebrews 13:8). We are secure in His hands when we commit our lives to Him.

God's faithfulness is evidence of His character. It shows us who God is and what He is like. God is faithful. He has always been

> **" GOD IS STABLE AND STEADFAST. HE DOESN'T CHANGE. "**

faithful. And He will always be faithful. His "faithfulness endures to all generations" (Psalm 119:90). We can trust God because He is constant; He will never be unfaithful.

So why do we have times when we doubt that God is faithful? Sometimes we forget. We focus on our circumstances, on what we are facing, instead of meditating on who God is and the victories He has already given us.

In the Bible, we see how Elijah did just that. Elijah was a prophet of God who challenged the 450 prophets of Baal. The challenge was designed to show that Elijah served the one, true God but that Baal was a false god (1 Kings 18). Elijah and Baal's prophets each put a bull sacrifice on wood without fire under it to see whose God would answer by fire (1 Kings 18:23-24).

Baal's prophets called on the name of Baal from morning to noon with no response (1 Kings 18:26). Then they cried aloud and cut themselves until evening, still without receiving any answer (1 Kings 18:28-29).

In the evening, Elijah built an altar in the name of the LORD, made a trench around the altar, put the wood on the altar and the bull on the wood, and then had the people pour 12 waterpots of water onto the bull and the wood so that the trench was filled with water (1 Kings 18:32-35). When Elijah called on the name of the LORD God, "the fire of the LORD fell and consumed the burnt sacrifice and the wood and the stones and the dust, and it licked up the water that was in the trench" (1 Kings 18:36-38).

What a remarkable victory that Elijah was privileged to experience! Despite witnessing this display of God's power, we later see Elijah discouraged, sitting under a tree, and praying that he might die (1 Kings 19:4). In a moment of despair, he had forgotten what God had done. Elijah had forgotten God's power and faithfulness.

We too can forget how God has been faithful in our lives. We need to build up our faith and our trust in God by remembering how He has already been faithful. When you meditate on the ways that God has been faithful in your life, you will be able to see His long history of faithfulness. You will remember how good He has been to you.

Because remembering God's faithfulness increases our faith, God has told us many times in the Bible to remember His works. "He has made His wonderful works to be remembered" (Psalm 111:4). We should "feed on His faithfulness" (Psalm 37:3). And when we purpose in our hearts to remember God's works, meditate on them, and talk about them, (Psalm 77:11-12) our hearts are encouraged and our faith is built up (Psalm 42:5, 11). We experience joy in what God has done and that joy strengthens us. As Nehemiah proclaimed, "[T]he joy of the LORD is your strength" (Nehemiah 8:10).

> **" GOD IS FAITHFUL IN THE SMALLEST OF DETAILS. "**

This book is about encouraging you to set up your own Ebenezer stones. Those stones will help you remember how God has been faithful in your life. God is faithful in the big, monumental things in our lives. And, God is faithful in the smallest of details.

Recently, I purchased a large glass jar and some stones. On each stone, I wrote a specific instance of God's faithfulness—some way He has helped me in my life—along with the date of the occurrence. The jar quickly began filling up as I remembered the things God had done for me and my family. Those instances included people He has saved and times of healing, provision, protection, guidance, and blessing. I could see God's hand in so much of my life.

I remembered the time God kept me from drowning when I was seven years old. I had been walking with my family on a pier in Atlantic City, New Jersey. One moment I was on the pier; the next moment I was in the ocean with the waves crashing over my head. Soon after, my dad and others jumped in to save me. By God's grace, no one was seriously harmed.

I thought about how God had provided for me after my parents divorced. There were times when it was difficult for my mom to afford the things that I needed. But God brought a benevolent man into my life who was like a father to me and who helped provide for me.

I meditated on how God had blessed me with my husband and my son. Both have brought me joy beyond measure. It has been a blessing to be able to walk alongside my husband over the years through life's ups and downs. And it was such a delight watching my son grow up. There are so many memories that I will always treasure—looking at his sweet face as a newborn, seeing him learn to walk, enjoying times of play, reading books to him, and teaching him different things. We know from the Bible that "[e]very good gift and every perfect gift is from above, and comes down from the Father of lights" (James 1:17).

As I remembered how God has been faithful in my life, my heart swelled with an overwhelming, deep contentedness and joy. When I doubt, I can go back to that jar and remind myself that God is faithful. I can build up my faith by remembering all the things He has done. "I will remember the works of the LORD; surely I will remember Your wonders of old. I will also meditate on all Your work and talk of Your deeds" (Psalm 77:11-12).

I hope as you read this book, you will see your Ebenezer stones. As you see them, set up those stones as a memorial to what God has done in your life. Take some stones and write on them the things God has done for you, along with the dates. Then place the stones where you will see them every day. When you see your Ebenezer stones, they will remind you how God has helped you. If you are having a difficult day, the sight of those stones will encourage you as you remember and meditate on God's faithfulness.

The stones will also create opportunities to tell others about what God has done for you. When someone sees them, they will wonder why you have a bunch of rocks. Their curiosity will give you a chance to tell them about the amazing things that God has done for you. He deserves all the glory.

Going Deeper

1. The feelings we experience are real. We all have them.

Although we may feel a certain way based on the circumstances we are facing, our feelings sometimes lie. Why was Elijah feeling discouraged? Read 1 Kings 19:14 and write down the answer.

2. Was Elijah's feeling true? Was he really the only one left? Read 1 Kings 19:18. How many people were still following God?

3. Determining whether our feelings are true can have a significant impact on our lives. "[A] lie believed as truth will affect your life as if it were true."[3] If you think something is true, you will live as if it is true, even if it's a lie.

If what we are feeling is not true, we can correct our wrong thinking. The Bible tells us to bring "every thought into captivity to the obedience of Christ" (2 Corinthians 10:5). When we do, we can determine if the feeling we are experiencing is based on something that is true or if it's a lie. If the feeling is based on a lie, by faith, we can hold on to the truth. We can meditate on what is actually true instead of the lie.

For example, have you ever told yourself that you are stupid or worthless? Maybe you did something that you shouldn't have done. You might have said the wrong thing at the wrong time, and you may need to stop that behavior and ask the person you wronged for forgiveness. But the action doesn't make you stupid or worthless. Take that thought captive. Don't let it continue to roll around in your mind.

Now, look at what the Bible tells you. The truth is that you are "fearfully and wonderfully made" (Psalm 139:14). The truth is that God made you a certain way. The truth is that God loves you (1 John 3:16). Meditate on the truth and not the lie.

Think back on your life to a time when you were discouraged. The feeling you experienced was real. But was the reason you were discouraged true?

Practice taking every thought captive. The next time you have a negative thought, stop yourself. Of course the feeling is real, but is what you are thinking true? Remember that we are all insecure or afraid sometimes, but our God is a faithful God.

4. Read 1 Samuel 7:7-12. How did God help the Israelites to defeat the Philistines?

God helped the Israelites, and He has helped you too. Journal about a way that God has helped you. Set up the Ebenezer stone to remind yourself about God's faithfulness. Thank God and praise Him for what He has done.

2

BECOMING A CHILD OF GOD

YOU CANNOT FULLY APPRECIATE THE FAITHFULNESS OF GOD IF you are not one of God's children. There is a widely held misconception that everyone is a child of God. I've heard many people say that we are all God's children. But that isn't true. While God does love everyone, we are not all His children.

Let me explain. Everyone was created by God. That is, we are all His creation. We were all physically born into this world. Each one of us has a body, soul, and spirit (1 Thessalonians 5:23). However, there is a difference between being physically born and spiritually born.

You can be physically alive but spiritually dead. It's not until you have been spiritually born that you become a child of God. Jesus said, to see the kingdom of God, we must be "born again" (John 3:3). He explained that a person cannot enter the kingdom of God unless he has been "born of water and the Spirit" (John 3:5). When you are born again, God adopts you as His child, and the Holy Spirit bears witness with your spirit that you are a child of God (Romans 8:15-16).

God wants each one of us to be born again, to be His child, so that we will enjoy eternal life with Him. We were made by God to be in a relationship with Him. God created us to enjoy fellowship with Him. But we have been separated from Him by sin.

God knew that we would be separated from Him—a separation so great that we wouldn't be able to make it back to Him on our own. So God devised a plan. God Himself would be our salvation. He would be the One who would save us from the penalty that comes from sin. God would make a way for us to come back to Him and have a relationship with Him. And God has been faithful to complete that plan of salvation.

God's Plan of Salvation

It began in the Garden of Eden. God had created Adam and Eve in His own image and placed them in the garden that He had made for them (Genesis 1:27, 2:7-8, 21-23). And God blessed them (Genesis 1:28) and everything was "very good" (Genesis 1:31). During that time, Adam and Eve enjoyed a relationship with God. They were innocent and did not know evil.

But that time didn't last. God had commanded them not to eat of the tree of the knowledge of good and evil (Genesis 2:17). Eventually, Adam and Eve sinned by disobeying God and eating from that tree (Genesis 3:1-6).

The word sin means "to miss the mark."[1] The term finds its roots in archery. When the archer misses the bullseye of the target (the mark), he sins.[2] Here, God set the "mark"—not eating from that tree—and Adam and Eve sinned by disregarding what God had told them.

After they sinned, the sweet fellowship they had with God was broken. And, "when they heard the sound of the LORD God walking in the garden," they hid themselves because they realized that they were naked (Genesis 3:8-11). Their innocence had been lost. Thankfully, God had a plan.

To understand that plan, we must first recognize that the only way to pay the penalty for sin is the shedding of blood. Blood makes atonement for the soul because "the life of the flesh is in the blood" (Leviticus 17:11). The Bible tells us that "the wages of sin is death" (Romans 6:23). Without the shedding of blood, there is no remission (forgiveness) of sin (Hebrews 9:22). We see the first sacrifice when God made "tunics of skin" for Adam and Eve to clothe them (Genesis 3:21). Sin always brings death.

In the Old Testament, it tells us how God set apart a group of people to be His, called the Israelites, and gave them a way to cover (atone) for their sin. The Israelites sacrificed certain animals to atone for their sin (Leviticus 16). But that atonement was temporary. It only cleansed the Israelites of their sin for a time, and they had to make atonement every year (Leviticus 16:34).

But God had a plan for a sacrifice that would only need to be made once to cleanse everyone from all of their sin. That plan required a perfect sacrifice. Only a perfect sacrifice could pay the penalty for sinning against a perfect, all-powerful God.

Yet, none of us is perfect. We all fall short of God's glory (Romans 3:23). We have all "missed the mark." For that reason, we could never do enough good works to pay the penalty for our own sin. Instead, the *best* works that we do are "filthy rags" in the eyes of God (Isaiah 64:6).

So God needed to provide the sacrifice for us. God has been faithful throughout history to provide that sacrifice—the One who would pay for the penalty of our sin and reconcile us to Him. Throughout the Old Testament, God foretold what He would do. There are prophesies in the Old Testament that tell us about the coming Savior (Messiah) who would suffer and die for everyone's sins (*see, e.g.,* Isaiah 53). All of those prophecies were fulfilled in Jesus (Hebrews 9:21-28).

The name Jesus is the English translation of His Hebrew name, Yeshua. The name Yeshua literally means salvation.[3] God sent His Son, Jesus, to die on the cross for our sins. Not just for my sins and your sins, but for everyone's sins. The Bible tells us, "For God so loved the world that He gave His only begotten Son, that whoever believes in Him should not perish but have everlasting life" (John 3:16).

> ❝ **JESUS IS THE WAY—THE ONLY WAY TO THE FATHER.** ❞

Jesus came down from heaven and became flesh so He could live a perfect, sinless life and sacrifice Himself for us (John 1:14; 2 Corinthians 5:21). He willingly laid down His own life (John 10:17-18). Jesus' sacrifice was perfect and only needed to be "offered once to bear the sins of many" (Hebrews 9:28). That's why Jesus is *the* way—the only way to the Father (John 14:6).

This New Covenant was also foretold in the Old Testament. Jeremiah prophesied,

> Behold, the days are coming, says the LORD, when I will make a new covenant with the house of Israel and with the

house of Judah—not according to the covenant that I made with their fathers in the day that I took them by the hand to lead them out of the land of Egypt, My covenant which they broke, though I was a husband to them, says the LORD. But this is the covenant that I will make with the house of Israel after those days, says the LORD: I will put My law in their minds, and write it on their hearts; and I will be their God, and they shall be My people.

No more shall every man teach his neighbor, and every man his brother, saying, "Know the LORD," for they all shall know Me, from the least of them to the greatest of them, says the LORD. For I will forgive their iniquity, and their sin I will remember no more. (Jeremiah 31:31-34)

Under this New Covenant, God would cast our sins as far as the east is from the west (Psalm 103:12), and He would remember them no more (Hebrews 10:17). How beautiful it is to know that all of our sins can be forgiven if we just humble ourselves to accept God's free gift of salvation, believing on the Lord Jesus Christ for the price He paid for our sins. I praise God for His amazing love—that He did what I could never have done on my own.

My Ebenezer Stone of Salvation

God was patient and faithful to bring me to Himself. It took many years for me to finally accept His free gift of salvation. He waited for me to come to the end of myself, until I finally surrendered to Him.

During my childhood, my family went to a variety of churches. I was christened in the Lutheran church as a baby and then attended Lutheran, Methodist, Presbyterian, and Baptist churches as I grew up. We even went to a Mormon "church"[4] at one point. It was primarily in the Baptist churches that I remember learning about Jesus.

By the time I was a teenager, we were attending a Baptist church. At Bible camp one summer, the pastor gave a "fire and brimstone" sermon. I remember being very afraid of dying and going to hell. So, when the pastor asked if there was anyone who wanted to accept Jesus, I made a confession of faith and was baptized a few weeks later. But there were no changes in my life. I didn't start reading the Bible, and I soon even stopped going to church.

A few years later, I was questioning the validity of the Bible (even though I hadn't read much of it), engaging in the party scene, and making up my own life and (so I thought) reality. I believed in the power of the mind. I thought you could shape your own destiny.

The further I got from God, the more wretched I became. Before I got married, I attended church again for a short period of time, but I still didn't believe. I knew the gospel (the good news about what Jesus had done for me). Yet, I was unwilling to submit myself to God, to do things His way.

Instead, I became a goal-setter, working toward certain ideals that I believed were important. I thought if I worked hard enough, I could control everything around me.

Years later, I came to a place where I had achieved most of my goals, and my life looked like I thought it should. I was married and had a child. I had a dog, a house, and a car I really liked. I was in great physical shape, ran, went on vacations some people only dream about, and did cool things like scuba diving. I had graduated from law school and was working at a law firm where I made a decent salary.

And I was miserable. Unsatisfied. I wondered, "Is this all there is to life? What's the point if you get this far and still feel empty inside?"

During this time, a friend gave me Lee Strobel's book, *The Case for Christ*. At the time he wrote the book, Strobel was a legal affairs journalist. After his wife started following Jesus, he investigated the life, death, and resurrection of Jesus. Strobel searched for evidence to either support or refute the validity of the Bible's claims. When he started the investigation, Strobel was an atheist. By the time he finished writing the book, he was a born-again believer.[5]

The book made sense to me; it was logical. There is evidence for the Bible, for Jesus, for the one, true God. After reading that book, I began to read the Bible. I wanted to read it cover-to-cover.

> " GOD PROMISES THAT WHEN YOU SEARCH FOR HIM WITH ALL YOUR HEART, YOU WILL FIND HIM. "

I was truly seeking God with all my heart for the first time in my life. God promises that when you search for Him with all your heart, you will find Him (Deuteronomy 4:29; Jeremiah 29:13).

As I was seeking Him, I came to a place where I hit an all-time low in my life. Not only did I feel empty inside, my job had become a drudgery. The law firm I worked for encouraged practices that were borderline (and sometimes over-the-line) unethical that I refused to participate in. I wanted out, felt trapped in the web of my own making, and didn't know what to do.

I prayed.

Even though I wasn't following God, I still prayed from time to time—like when I was afraid for my son's or my husband's safety. This time was different. The prayer I prayed wasn't necessarily a good prayer, but I meant it. And God is so gracious to meet us where we're at. I promised God that if He got me out of the job I was in, I would start going to church.

That very afternoon, I got an email from a judge I had worked for, telling me that one of the other judge's law clerks was leaving early and needed someone to fill in. By the following afternoon, I had the job.

I was amazed at how quickly it happened, pretty much immediately after my prayer. It left no doubt in my mind that it was God's handiwork. I knew I had to do what I had promised God I'd do in return. I had to go to church. The problem was that my husband and I had been married for 16 years but, other than getting married in one, we had never gone to church together. And we had never even talked about going.

When I went home that night, I walked in the door and casually asked my husband, "So, do you want to go to church this weekend?" I expected push back or at least some trepidation. Instead, to my surprise, he answered, "Sure."

God is amazing. Looking back, I realized that God was not only preparing my heart to come to Him, but my husband's heart as well.

That Sunday, we went to church, and I gave my life to God. No fanfare. No fear. No altar call. No message about sinners going to hell. It was just me and God. He is so good to me. He waited so patiently, gently drawing me to Himself. He is my beautiful Savior, the faithful One—my God.

Your Salvation Stone

Do you have the Ebenezer stone of salvation in your life? If you don't, I pray that you will humble yourself and accept God's free gift of salvation. We are not guaranteed tomorrow. Today is the day of salvation (2 Corinthians 6:2).

In the Old Testament, God gave the ten commandments to the Israelites (Exodus 20:1-17). The ten commandments are some of the "marks" that God has set for each one of us to reach. If you have broken any of those commandments, you have missed the mark and have sinned.

For example, have you ever told a lie? God commands us to refrain from lying (Exodus 20:16). If you have ever told a lie, then you have sinned. We like to justify our sin so it doesn't sound so bad. You may say, "Well it was only a little, white lie." But God sets the standards, not us. And a lie is a lie.

If you accept God's free gift of salvation, He will forgive all of your sins. But dying without accepting the gift of salvation is the one unforgivable sin called the blasphemy of the Holy Spirit (Matthew 12:31-32). The sin is unforgivable because Jesus is the *only* way to be reconciled to God. If you reject Jesus, you are rejecting His work of dying on the cross for your sin. Without anything to pay the penalty for your sin, you will be judged by God for that sin. And the wages of your sin is death (Romans 6:23).

The Bible tells us that "it is appointed for men to die once, but after this the judgment" (Hebrews 9:27). God gives you the free will to decide whether you want to be with Him. You must make the choice to accept Jesus as your Savior before you die. If you die while you are still separated from God, you will remain eternally separated from Him. In that separation,

Jesus said there will be weeping and gnashing of teeth (Matthew 8:12). But God is "longsuffering toward us, not willing that any should perish" (2 Peter 3:9).

Moreover, the promises that God has made to His children can be enjoyed by every child of God. But you cannot rely on them until you become His child. So, how do you become a child of God?

As we saw earlier, we know that "all have sinned and fall short of the glory of God" (Romans 3:23). But praise God that He demonstrated "His own love toward us, in that while we were still sinners, Christ died for us" (Romans 5:8). And three days later, God raised Jesus from the dead (Matthew 28:6). Jesus overcame death! By doing so, God gave us the gift of "eternal life in Christ Jesus our Lord" (Romans 6:23).

This gift is free. However, as with any gift, a person must accept the gift to enjoy it. To do that, you need only "confess with your mouth the Lord Jesus and believe in your heart that God has raised Him from the dead" (Romans 10:9). "For 'whoever calls on the name of the LORD shall be saved'" (Romans 10:13 (quoting Joel 2:32)).

> **COME TO JESUS AS YOU ARE.**

In calling on His name, you are agreeing that you are a sinner in need of a Savior and you need Him to pay the penalty of your sin. It's a confession that you know you need Jesus and have decided to follow Him.

Because your best works are like filthy rags, you don't need to clean yourself up before you come to Jesus. There are some who think they need to get their lives in order before they decide to follow Jesus. Come to Jesus as you are. After you become God's child, He will change you. He will clean you up. It's His work, not your own.

Once you make the decision to turn away from your sinful life and confess that Jesus is Lord over your life, you are born again. If you are born again, you are God's child. As the Bible tells us, "[A]s many as received Him, to them He gave the right to become children of God, to those who believe in His name" (John 1:12). Isn't that amazing? Not only *can* you become a child of God but your belief in Jesus gives you a *right* to be His child. "Behold what manner of love the Father has bestowed on us, that we should be called children of God!" (1 John 3:1).

I hope that you either have chosen or will choose to accept God's free gift of salvation—that you will accept Jesus and have the Ebenezer stone of salvation in your life. If you have, lift up the stone as a memorial to remind you that God has forgiven all of your sins and has cast them as far as the east is from the west. He has given you a fresh start and made you a "new creation" (2 Corinthians 5:17). Glorify God by telling others what He has done for you. Be bold and share your testimony with the people God has placed in your life.

Going Deeper

1. We can make up our own expectations about what we think is right. But what really matters is what God tells us is right or wrong. In the Bible, God tells us about the "marks" he has set for each one of us. God gave the Israelites the ten

commandments as some of those standards. In this chapter, we talked about one of them, lying. Read Exodus 20:1-17 and write down the other nine commandments that God gave them.

2. Have you ever broken any of the "marks" that God has set? Be honest with yourself. Write down one way you have missed God's marks.

3. Are you born again?

If you are born again, journal about your testimony. Write down how God brought you to Him. Share your testimony with someone this week.

If not, what is holding you back? Consider your reasons for not accepting God's free gift. Do you have questions? Journal about your reasons and/or questions. Then tell God about those reasons and ask Him to answer your questions. You might be surprised about what God does if you genuinely come to Him seeking the truth.

3

GROWING IN SPIRITUAL MATURITY

AFTER WE MAKE THE DECISION TO FOLLOW JESUS, HE forgives us of all our sins (Colossians 2:13-14). But even though we have a relationship with God, we still sin. We still have our human nature—called the "flesh" in the Bible (Romans 8:5)—with all of its "moral frailties and passions."[1] And our flesh is contrary to the Holy Spirit who lives inside of us (Galatians 5:17). For that reason, we continue to be tempted to sin.

It is important to remember that the temptation itself is not a sin. Jesus was tempted (Matthew 4:1-10); yet, we know that He remained sinless (Hebrews 4:15). It's only when you act on the temptation that you sin. Unfortunately, we do continue to act on temptations.

But God is faithful to change us into the image of Jesus. As He changes us, we will grow in spiritual maturity. You will know He is changing you when you see more of the "fruit of the Spirit" in your life. That fruit is "love, joy, peace, longsuffering, kindness, goodness, faithfulness, gentleness, [and] self-control" (Galatians 5:22-23).

Likewise, you will see less of the works of the flesh (Galatians 5:19). While we are alive, we will not be sinless. But we will sin less. The Bible lists the types of things that come from our flesh and are contrary to God. Those works of the flesh include "adultery, fornication, uncleanness, lewdness, idolatry, sorcery, hatred, contentions, jealousies, outbursts of wrath, selfish ambitions, dissensions, heresies, envy, murders, drunkenness, revelries, and the like" (Galatians 5:19-21).

Look back on your life since you started following Jesus. You will likely notice a difference in your attitude, the types of shows you watch on tv, and how you spend your time. There will be a difference in the things that are important to you. If you see any of the works of the flesh in your life (and if you are honest with yourself, you will still see them), remember that God is working to change you as you yield to His authority.

God is the Potter, and we are the clay in His hands. In Genesis 2:7, we see that when God created man, he "formed man of the dust of the ground, and breathed into his nostrils the breath of life; and man became a living being." The transliteration of the Hebrew word "formed" is yasar, which means to mold into a form, "especially as a potter."[2]

The same Hebrew word (yasar) is used in Jeremiah 18, when the Lord told Jeremiah to go to the potter's house, where he would hear God's words. Jeremiah went there and saw the potter "making something at the wheel" (Jeremiah 18:2-3). "And the vessel that he made of clay was marred in the hand of the potter; so he made it again into another vessel, as it seemed good to the potter to make" (Jeremiah 18:4). As we read further, we learn that God is the Potter, and Israel is the clay in His hands (Jeremiah 18:6).

Just as Israel was in His hands, we too are the clay in God's hands. As the wheel of your life turns and you are

> **GOD IS THE POTTER, AND WE ARE THE CLAY IN HIS HANDS.**

marred (ruined), you can be comforted in knowing that you are in God's hands. And He is shaping you into another vessel as it seems good to Him to make. As the Bible says, "But now, O LORD, You are our Father; we are the clay, and You our potter [yasar]; and all we are the work of Your hand" (Isaiah 64:8).

It's awesome to think about. It's not my work or yours. It's God's work, and He will finish what He started. The Bible tells us that you can be "confident" that "He who has begun a good work in you will complete it" (Philippians 1:6).

Who am I to ask my Potter, my Creator, what He is doing or why He is doing it? "Shall the clay say to him who forms it, 'What are you making?'" (Isaiah 45:9). And yet I sometimes do just that.

I may not directly question why He is doing something in my life. Instead, I come up with my own plans and then get frustrated when things don't go the way I think they should. I am so thankful that God is ready to forgive me, each time I see the error of my ways, turn away from my sin, and turn towards God (repent). "If we confess our sins, He is faithful and just to forgive us our sins and to cleanse us from all unrighteousness" (1 John 1:9). Praise God!

God uses the difficulties in our lives to change us into Jesus' image. The Bible refers to those difficulties as trials. The Bible teaches us that we will have trials in our lives (James 1:2) and not to think it strange when we go through them (1 Peter 4:12). Those trials may come as a result of our own or someone else's actions (or failure to act) or from living a Christian life. There are also trials that don't make sense. From our perspective, we cannot see the reason for them.

Regardless of the source of the trial, God can use it to help us grow in spiritual maturity. For example, God may use a trial to reveal whether our faith is genuine, to correct us, or to perfect us.

Revealing Trials

The Bible shows us that a trial will reveal the foundation that we are building our lives on. Jesus told us,

> Therefore whoever hears these sayings of Mine, and does them, I will liken him to a wise man who built his house on the rock: and the rain descended, the floods came, and the winds blew and beat on that house; and it did not fall, for it was founded on the rock.
>
> But everyone who hears these sayings of Mine, and does not do them, will be like a foolish man who built his house on the sand: and the rain descended, the floods came, and the winds blew and beat on that house; and it fell. And great was its fall. (Matthew 7:24-27)

We must build our lives on Jesus, the solid Rock. We do that by learning about what God wants us to do and then applying what we learn. As James told us, "be doers of the word, and not hearers only, deceiving yourselves" (James 1:22).

When you build your life on the principles that Jesus taught, a trial will reveal that your faith is genuine. In other words, you won't stop following Jesus when things get tough. Instead, you will lean into Jesus, relying on Him to get you through the trial. As Peter said,

> In this you greatly rejoice, though now for a little while, if need be, you have been grieved by various trials, that the genuineness of your faith, being much more precious than gold that perishes, though it is tested by fire, may be found to praise, honor, and glory at the revelation of Jesus Christ, whom having not seen you love. (1 Peter 1:6-8)

Some people appear to be following Jesus. They go to church every week and say all the right things. But when they go through a trial, they walk away from God. The trial reveals that their faith wasn't genuine. As Pastor Greg Laurie put it, "[I]f someone says they lost their faith because of a certain crisis, then I would say that's good, because they need to get rid of that faith. It's worthless. The faith that cannot be tested is a faith that cannot be trusted."[3]

Correcting Trials

God uses trials to correct us. In the Bible, we see that God used a trial to correct Jonah. Jonah was one of God's prophets. When God told Jonah to go and preach to the Ninevites, Jonah refused and got on a boat that was going to a place in the opposite direction from where the Ninevites lived (Jonah 1:1-3). God brought a big storm that threatened the lives of all who were on the boat (Jonah 1:4-5). After they tossed Jonah overboard, the storm ceased (Jonah 1:12, 15).

But the trial wasn't over for Jonah. God had prepared a large fish to swallow him (Jonah 1:17). When Jonah finally repented three days later, the big fish expelled him onto dry land (Jonah 1:17-2:10).

The lesson to learn from Jonah is that we should obey God's commands. We can learn about how God wants us to live by reading the Bible. The Bible is God's Word. It is "inspired by God and is useful to teach us what is true and to make us realize what is wrong in our lives. It corrects us when we are wrong and teaches us to do what is right" (2 Timothy 3:16 (NLT)).

When you don't obey God, you can expect that He will correct you. The Bible tells us that God disciplines His children (Hebrews 12:6). Although no one enjoys correction while it is happening, "afterward it yields the peaceable fruit of righteousness to those who have been trained by it" (Hebrews 12:11).

Perfecting Trials

God also uses trials to perfect us. James tells us to "count it all joy when you fall into various trials, knowing that the testing of your faith produces patience" (James 1:2-3). The Greek word for patience is hypomone, which means "steadfastness, constancy, endurance."[4] The trials in our lives make our faith more resolute and stable, strengthening our faith in Jesus.

When we see firsthand how God is faithful to us during a trial, our trust in Him grows. As it does, our faith is built up.

We are even able to rest in the middle of the trial because we know that God will be there for us.

This patience that is produced by the testing of our faith perfects us. As we read further, James teaches us, "But let patience have its perfect work, that you may be perfect and complete, lacking nothing" (James 1:4). The word perfect means "brought to its end, finished."[5] God uses the trials we go through to finish the work He started in us.

Trials help us become more spiritually mature. As Pastor Jon Courson noted, "Maturity only comes through testing. Faith is made pure only when fiery trials burn away the dross."[6] It's only when we remember that God is using the trial to perfect us that we can "count it all joy."

A Global Trial

I can look back and see the things God used in my life to change me. It has been a process of becoming less prideful, selfish, and angry, and more loving, patient, and kind. Sometimes He has used a verse from the Bible that resulted in small moments of realization or chastisement. Other times were more monumental. Regardless of the size of the trial, God used it for some purpose.

In early 2020, a virus began rapidly spreading throughout the world. The name of the virus, COVID-19, became a familiar name. Soon, scientists realized that the virus was highly contagious and fatal to some. Practically overnight, all of our lives changed.

As hospitals were filling up, governments issued stay-at-home orders. Schools were closed. Businesses deemed non-essential temporarily closed. Restaurants only remained open for takeout and delivery. Millions of people lost their jobs, and the stock market fell. Gatherings of any kind outside the family living unit were prohibited. Everyone around the world was going through the same trial, albeit with different levels of impact on their lives.

So far, the Lord had sheltered us from much of it. I had been required to work from home for months and my husband was working from home part of the time as well. Going out to the grocery store once a week for food and supplies had become an adventure. Certain items were hard to find, especially at the start of the pandemic.

Before the trial, I took it for granted that when I wanted to buy things—like toilet paper, cleaning supplies, canned food, flour, and yeast—I could go to the store and there would be numerous brands, well-stocked to choose from. But since the trial had started, those things may or may not be in stock at the store. And if the store had it, you might only have a single option. People were fearful, so they hoarded supplies and non-perishable food.

God had allowed the virus. Did I understand why? No. Yet, in the midst of it all, I could already see some by-products of the trial.

The stay-at-home orders had forced families to be together. Families that had their lives plagued by busyness, some barely able to find time to eat dinner together, were now spending time with each other. Through my window, I watched parents playing with their children in their yards.

After the schools closed, they eventually started providing materials online, along with some class time. But parents were now responsible for teaching their children and saw firsthand the content of the school's curriculum.

Churches were not allowed to gather in most places in groups of more than ten. Suddenly, churches were streaming services. Churches were having Bible studies and meetings online. The church was being brought into people's homes.

Most importantly, people had more time to think. When the busyness stops, you are forced to look deeper. People who otherwise would not have made the time to think about God were doing just that. And those who already had a relationship with God were given more time to focus on Him. Time had been freed up to spend in fellowship with our faithful, loving God.

Also, the trial revealed the foundation that each of us had been building on. It became evident where you had placed your trust. Had you placed your hope in entertainment? Pleasure? Your job? Your bank account or stock portfolio? Or had you built your life on the Rock, the One who is in control of everything?

God used the trial in my life to draw me even closer to Him. Before the trial, it seemed that we were always busy. I would get up early, commute to work, spend nine hours at work, and then commute home. Several nights during the week, we were busy with Bible studies, small group meetings, and a mid-week church service. Each of those things required a commute. Weekends were just as busy with church services, serving at our church, errands, chores, and occasional family gatherings. These were good things. But it seemed there was always so much to do with little time to really stop and think.

After the trial started, life slowed down. I no longer had to commute to work, and we could no longer worship at our church or gather together for Bible studies. Even though we still participated in our church services and Bible study online, there was suddenly time—unexpected, sweet time. Time to pray in the morning. Time to think and meditate on God's word. Time to listen to God speak to me.

God showed me a lot during that time. He showed me how I was still holding on to my own plans instead of completely surrendering to His plans for me. He revealed that I was actually afraid of relenting to His plan, that I had not been wholly trusting in Him. It was a beautiful time of deepening my dependence on God, knowing that He is stronger.

God also showed me that He is not making me into what seems good to me but what seems good to Him. That's why it's important to let go of our own plans when they don't line up with the plans God has for us. Besides, God's plans are always better than our own plans. Sometimes we delay the joy we will receive from a plan that God has for us when we tightly hold on to our own plan rather than submitting to His plan.

❝ GOD'S PLANS ARE ALWAYS BETTER THAN OUR OWN PLANS. ❞

Recently, I was reading in the book of Genesis about Jacob. Jacob had twelve sons, but he "loved Joseph more than all his children, because he was the son of his old age" (Genesis 37:3). The favoritism Jacob showed to Joseph caused Joseph's brothers to hate Joseph (Genesis 37:4). Their animosity grew until they sold Joseph into slavery and led Jacob to believe that Joseph had died (Genesis 37:28, 31-34). When he thought Joseph was dead, Jacob refused to be comforted (Genesis 37:35).

As we fast forward about 20 years, we see that God has taken Joseph out of slavery and raised him into the second in command of Egypt (Genesis 41:38-43). There was a great famine, but Egypt had plenty of grain in its storehouses because of the wisdom God had bestowed on Joseph (Genesis 41:47-49, 54). So, the surrounding countries went to Joseph in Egypt to buy grain (Genesis 41:57).

When Jacob heard that there was grain in Egypt, he sent all of his sons, except Benjamin (Joseph's younger brother), to buy grain (Genesis 42:1-4). He did not send Benjamin "[l]est some calamity befall him" (Genesis 42:4). Joseph recognized his brothers, but they did not recognize him (Genesis 42:8). Joseph saw that Benjamin was not with them, so he gave them some grain, put Simeon in prison, and told them to bring their youngest brother back with them (Genesis 42:19-20, 24-25).

When his sons returned, Jacob refused to allow them to take Benjamin to Egypt (Genesis 42:38). He tightly held on to Benjamin because of his sorrow and grief. Jacob was trying to control the situation. He didn't want to lose Benjamin after he had already lost Joseph.

By holding on to Benjamin, it delayed the blessing that God had for him. After he was willing to let go of Benjamin and put it in God's hands (Genesis 43:11-14), he was finally able to receive the fullness of joy that God had for him. Only then could he learn that Joseph was still alive and go to see him. Only then could his heart be revived (Genesis 45:26-28).

Then I looked at my own life. I hold on to things too. I had been holding on to the ideal of what I thought my life should have been like. I had come up with that ideal after I started following Jesus, and God showed me the things that are really important.

I was full of regret, wishing I could go back and change things into how I thought they should have been. If my husband and I had come to the Lord earlier in life, we would have lived our lives very differently. We would have trained up our son in the way he should go. We might have had more children. But that ideal doesn't exist. And I can't go back in time.

Focusing on what might have been only wastes our time in the present. Living in the past (or what you wish the past would have been) delays you from receiving what God has for you now. You can't go back, but you can enjoy what God has for you today.

God has fashioned days for you (Psalm 139:16). He knew what you would do. His plans for you remain despite what you have done. You have not ruined them. Do you really think that you are powerful enough to change God's plans? As the apostle Paul would say, "Certainly not!"

God had used the COVID-19 trial to show me certain things. Because I am closer to Him now than when the trial started, I can be joyful in the trial. Still, I don't understand why the trial had to happen. And, I don't understand why the trial continues. You may not learn why you go through a trial, but you can be comforted by remembering certain truths found in the Bible.

First, as we saw earlier, God is using the trial to help you grow in spiritual maturity. God works all things "together for good to those who love God, to those who are the called according to His purpose. For whom He foreknew, He also predestined to be conformed to the image of His Son" (Romans 8:28-29). God is using the trial to change you into the image of Jesus.

Second, God is there when you cry out to Him. God is "near to all who call upon Him, to all who call upon Him in truth" (Psalm 145:18). He will never leave you or abandon you

(Hebrews 13:5). The Bible tells us that God is "near to those who have a broken heart" (Psalm 34:18). God is the one who "heals the brokenhearted and binds up their wounds" (Psalm 147:3). And, He hears every prayer (Psalm 18:6). He even puts your tears in a bottle (Psalm 56:8).

I praise God that He is always there to hear me. He never sleeps or slumbers (Psalm 121:4). Over time, He will heal your wounds.

Third, God is in control of everything. He is sovereign. The perception that we are in control of our lives is an illusion. Sure, we make choices, and choices have certain outcomes and consequences. And we can control the choices we make and how we respond to certain situations. Ultimately, however, we cannot control another person's choices and other things that happen in our lives.

But God made the heavens, the earth and everything on it; He made the seas and all that is in them; and He preserves them all (Nehemiah 9:6). He is holding everything together (Colossians 1:16-17). He even "changes the times and the seasons" (Daniel 2:21). God raises up one person into authority and removes another (Daniel 2:21), and He can control their decisions (Proverbs 21:1). God determines where each of us will be born and who our parents will be (Acts 17:26). God knows every choice you will make in your life, and He placed you where you are so that you are in the best place to seek Him "in the hope that [you] might grope for Him and find Him, though He is not far from each one of us" (Acts 17:27).

Finally, God's thoughts toward you are "more in number than the sand" (Psalm 139:18). His plans are not to harm you but to give you a future and a hope (Jeremiah 29:11). So, as

God works in your life to change you, you can trust Him. As the Bible tells us, "we all, with unveiled face, beholding as in a mirror the glory of the Lord, are being transformed into the same image from glory to glory, just as by the Spirit of the Lord" (2 Corinthians 3:18).

Going Deeper

1. Take time to reflect on your walk with Jesus. Do you see the fruit of the Spirit in your life? Are you more loving than when you first started following Him? Do you have more self-control? Are you more patient? Journal about the changes you see and thank God for the way He has changed you.

2. Have you been holding on to anything from your past or to what you wish your past could have been? If so, what have you been holding on to?

Paul showed us how to let go of the things in our past and

reach forward to the things that are ahead. After admitting that he had not already reached perfection, Paul told us,

> No, dear brothers and sisters, I have not achieved it, but I focus on this one thing: Forgetting the past and looking forward to what lies ahead, I press on to reach the end of the race and receive the heavenly prize for which God, through Christ Jesus, is calling us. (Philippians 3:13-14 (NLT))

To let go of the past, we must change the direction of our thinking from our past to the eternal. When we shift our thinking away from our past and toward God's future promises, we won't waste any more time. Instead, we can look forward to what God still has in store for us. Write out a prayer asking God to help you let go of your regret—to forget the past and focus on the plans He has for you today.

3. How has God used the COVID-19 trial in your life? What has He shown you? Are you more like Jesus now than when the trial began? In what ways?

4. Trials are a part of the Christian life. You are either

going through one, just came out of one, or about to go through one.

If you are in a trial, hang on to God. Stay close to Him. Jesus is going through the trial with you. Pray to God, read His word, and allow yourself to hear from Him. Jesus is the Rock who will get you through it. Write out a prayer asking God to help you through the trial.

If you are just coming out of a trial, praise God that He got you through it. Journal about what you learned in the trial and how God helped you. What type of trial was it? What did God show you during the trial? Set up your Ebenezer stone so you will remember how God helped you. Thank God and praise Him for what He has done in your life.

If you are not currently in a trial, prepare yourself by staying close to God. Jesus told us, "In the world you will have tribulation [trials]; but be of good cheer, I have overcome the world" (John 16:33). It's not a question of if you will go through a trial but when. Spend time every day with God, reading His word and praying to Him. Memorize verses from the Bible. When you are in a trial, God will use the verses you learned to help you. He will bring certain verses to your remembrance when you need them most. Write out a prayer for God to help you prepare for the next trial you will go through.

4

THE GOOD SHEPHERD

DIFFERENT PARTS OF THE BIBLE COMPARE PEOPLE TO SHEEP.
At first glance, it may seem like an endearing comparison.
After all, sheep are often portrayed in cartoons as cute and
fluffy. However, a closer look reveals that the analogy is not a
compliment. In reality, sheep are not the brightest of animals.
And they are stubborn. As W. Phillip Keller, who was a shepherd by trade, described,

> Sheep are notorious creatures of habit. If left to themselves,
> they will follow the same trails until they become ruts; graze
> the same hills until they turn to desert wastes; pollute their
> own ground until it is corrupt with disease and parasites.[1]

Sheep follow each other around without thinking for
themselves. In 2005, a Turkish newspaper reported that shep-
herds had watched "in horror" as hundreds of sheep followed
each other over a cliff. After one sheep went over the edge, it
was followed by the entire flock. More than 400 sheep died

after falling almost 50 feet. The sheep that died cushioned the fall of the remaining 1,100 sheep that followed.[2]

Moreover, sheep have no way of defending themselves from predators or protecting themselves from parasites; they sometimes stray from the flock; and they are unable to ensure that they have food to eat and water to drink. Over the years, the occasional news story tells us about rogue sheep that have escaped their pens and wandered away from the flock. When found, the sheep were on the brink of death, having become infested with parasites, malnourished, and overgrown with wool to the extent they can barely walk.

One such sheep, nicknamed Chris, was found in Australia after wandering for about seven years. It took 42 minutes to remove the excess wool, which weighed 89 pounds.[3] When rescuers found another sheep, called Baarack, it was underweight and could barely see due to the wool around its face.[4] Sheep need a shepherd, someone to protect them, care for them, keep them from straying, and ensure that they are well-fed and watered.

In Psalm 23, David compares himself to a sheep, acknowledging that God is his Shepherd.

> The LORD is my Shepherd; I shall not want. He makes me to lie down in green pastures; He leads me beside the still waters. He restores my soul; He leads me in the paths of righteousness for His name's sake. Yea, though I walk through the valley of the shadow of death, I will fear no evil; for You are with me; Your rod and Your staff, they comfort me. You prepare a table before me in the presence of my enemies; You anoint my head with oil; my cup runs over. Surely goodness and mercy shall follow me all the days

of my life; and I will dwell in the house of the LORD forever.
(Psalm 23)

David penned this familiar, beautiful prose under the guidance of the Holy Spirit. He uses the illustration of a shepherd to teach us about God's guidance, provision, and protection. We learn from Jesus that He is the good Shepherd that David was talking about (John 10:14-16). Jesus was moved with compassion when He saw the multitudes of people "because they were weary and scattered, like sheep having no shepherd" (Matthew 9:36).

Without Jesus, we too are like sheep without a shepherd. Left to our own devices, we stubbornly follow the same paths even when

> **WE ALL NEED THE GOOD SHEPHERD, JESUS.**

it is harmful to us. We do things our friends do without first thinking about the consequences because we want to fit in and feel like we belong. We stray from doing what is right. Instead of doing what God wants us to do, we do what we want to do without any consideration of God. The Bible teaches us, "All we like sheep have gone astray; we have turned, every one, to his own way" (Isaiah 53:6). We stray like sheep.

We all need the good Shepherd, Jesus. When we personalize Psalm 23, we too can look at ourselves as sheep with Jesus as our Shepherd. Just as sheep need a shepherd, we need God to guide us, provide for us, and protect us. As you follow the good Shepherd, you can know that God will be faithful to provide for you, guide you, and protect you.

Provision

God is faithful to provide for our physical needs. He may not give us everything we *want*, but He will give us everything we need (Philippians 4:19). Knowing that God will provide for our needs, we should be content with what we have.

We sometimes confuse the things we want with the things we actually need. When we want something a lot, we may convince ourselves that we need it, even when we don't. The Bible gives us perspective about what is necessary. That viewpoint is different from what you might otherwise think. As Paul tells us in 1 Timothy 6:7-8, "For we brought nothing into this world, and it is certain we can carry nothing out. And having food and clothing, with these we shall be content."

Thankfully, God has provided much more than just food and clothing for most of us. We should be content with the abundance of God's provision.

Often, when we have a need, we worry about how we will take care of it. Perhaps the rent is due in a week, and you don't have the money to pay for it. Or maybe you have been out of work and haven't been able to find a job.

Jesus instructed us not to worry or be anxious about our needs (Matthew 6:25-32). Jesus reminded us, "Which of you by worrying can add one cubit to his stature?" (Matthew 6:27). As the New Living Translation phrases it, "Can all your worries add a single moment to your life?" Instead of worrying, we should seek God first, and He will provide what we need (Matthew 6:33).

Yet, what we should do is not what we always do. God recognizes that we worry and become anxious about our needs. In His grace, He gives us further instruction about how to obtain peace while we wait on Him to provide for our needs. The Bible tells us,

> Be anxious for nothing, but in everything by prayer and supplication, with thanksgiving, let your requests be made known to God; and the peace of God, which surpasses all understanding, will guard your hearts and minds through Christ Jesus. (Philippians 4:6-7)

So, we should ask God to supply our needs by prayer and supplication, with thanksgiving. "In this context, prayer refers to communing with God, while supplication speaks of making specific requests to Him."[5]

The way to get rid of your anxiety and worry is by spending time with God, telling Him about your needs, and asking Him to provide for them. You can talk to God and tell Him how you are feeling. He won't be surprised by anything you have to say.

Then thank God for all that He has already done in your life. He has done many great things for each one of us. He has saved us, forgiven our sins, and provided for us in big and small ways. He gives us the very breath in our lungs. Pull out your Ebenezer stones, meditate on what God has done, and praise Him for those things. You can also meditate on the promises God gives us about what He will do in the future. Search the Bible for those promises and cling to them.

When we come to God with our needs and a thankful heart, He promises to give us peace. That peace is "of God" and "surpasses all understanding" (Philippians 4:7). It is not a worldly idea of peace. It's a supernatural peace that only comes from God. As Jesus told us, "Peace I leave with you, My peace I give to you; not as the world gives do I give to you. Let not your heart be troubled, neither let it be afraid" (John 14: 27). Peace from the world can come and go at any moment. But the peace Jesus offers is there whenever you need it. You just need to go to Him and trust Him so you can receive it.

Memorize the verses in Philippians so you can remember God's remedy to your worry and anxiety no matter where you are or what you are doing. Go to God as often as you need to. The Bible tells us, "Cast your burden on the LORD, and He shall sustain you" (Psalm 55:22). The word cast means to throw, hurl, or fling.[6] God doesn't want you to sort of hand it over to Him and then take it back. Instead, God tells you to throw it to Him. When you do, it's out of your hands. He has it and will handle it for you.

Some days, you may need to go to God moment by moment. As you do, you can take comfort in knowing that God knows the things you need before you even ask Him (Matthew 6:8). God knows the details of your life so that even all of the hairs on your head are numbered (Matthew 10:30).

We don't tell God about our needs because He doesn't know about them. The reason we do so is for our benefit. God wants us to tell Him about the things we are worried about because He knows we aren't able to handle everything on our own. God wants us to cast all our cares on Him because He cares for us (1 Peter 5:7).

In addition to bringing your needs to God, you can build up your faith by meditating on the extraordinary ways that God provided for people in the Bible. The Bible gives us many examples of God's provision.

After God brought the Israelites out of bondage from Egypt and led them into the wilderness, the Israelites were thirsty and had no water to drink. Moses cried out to God on their behalf, and God supernaturally provided water for them to drink from a rock (Exodus 17:1-6). And, when the Israelites did not have anything to eat, God gave them food from heaven (Exodus 16:3-4).

We also see God providing food for the multitudes who followed Jesus onto a mountain, staying with Him for three days. Jesus had compassion on them, knowing that they had nothing to eat. He didn't want to send them away hungry "lest they faint on the way" (Matthew 15:29-32).

So, Jesus took the little they had (a few little fish and seven small loaves of bread), gave thanks, broke them, and gave them to His disciples to distribute to the multitude (Matthew 15:34-36). God multiplied those few fish and seven loaves so that 4,000 men (plus the women and children who were there but were not counted) were filled (Matthew 15:37-38). Not only were they filled, but there were seven large baskets of fragments left over (Matthew 15:37).

Examples of God's provision are not limited to what we see in the Bible. There are numerous illustrations of God's provision in church history. In the 1800s, George Muller was called by God to start several orphanages in Bristol, England. Throughout his work, he never requested financial support from others or went into debt. Instead, he constantly prayed to God for all of their needs, and God supplied them.

On one occasion, all of the children were sitting at the table and thanks was given to God for breakfast even though they had nothing to eat. As they finished praying, the baker knocked on the door with enough bread to feed everyone. And the milkman gave them fresh milk to drink because his cart had broken down in front of the orphanage.[7]

God is awesome. He can provide in ways we would never think of. He is bigger than any problem you have. Don't look at the size of your problem or need in comparison to your own ability. Instead, look at it in relation to the size of your God, the Creator of the universe. Go to Him. Tell God what you need and then meditate on His faithfulness as you wait on Him.

Guidance

God is faithful to lead and guide us. As we navigate through our lives, we know that God will be there when we turn to Him for direction.

In the Old Testament, we see that God led the Israelites while they were in the wilderness in a unique way. By day, God went before them in a pillar of cloud. And by night, He used a pillar of fire to guide them (Exodus 13:21). The pillar of cloud or fire was always there (Exodus 13:22). When the pillar of cloud or fire moved, the Israelites followed.

Sometimes it seems like it would be nice if God led us in that way. We could just watch the pillar of cloud or fire, knowing with certainty that God wants us to follow it whenever it moves. But the truth is that God has given us something better. He has given us His word (the Bible) and the Holy Spirit to guide us (John 14:16).

God's word is "a lamp to [our] feet and a light to [our] path" (Psalm 119:105). It gives us "instruction in righteousness" (2 Timothy 3:16). God tells us how He wants us to live. For example, in Titus 2:12, we are told to deny "ungodliness and worldly lusts" and that we "should live soberly, righteously, and godly." When you are looking for guidance from

God, one of the first things you should do is open the Bible to
see if the thing you are thinking about doing is something that
God told us not to do.

If you are thinking about robbing a bank, it will quickly
become clear to you that God doesn't want you to do that
because He has commanded us not to steal (Exodus 20:15).
Of course, that's a pretty simplistic example. Most people are
not thinking about robbing a bank. But what about that long
lunch hour that you took at work? Are you going to make up
that time? Or will you just brush it off like it's no big deal
because everyone else does it? Getting paid for time you didn't
work is a form of stealing.

Or what if you are married but have reconnected on social
media with a guy that you used to know and wonder if you
should leave your husband to be with him. After all, he seems
to listen to your every thought, while your husband is always
distracted and self-centered. A look in the Bible shows us that
Jesus said doing so would be committing adultery (Mark
10:12).

The more time we spend in the Bible, the better we will
know what God wants us to do. Jesus told us, "My sheep hear
My voice, and I know them, and they follow Me" (John
10:27).

God also leads us with the Holy Spirit. When you are born
again, the Holy Spirit comes to live inside of you (John 14:16-
17) and helps you to understand what God wants you to do.
As Paul taught us, "we have received, not the spirit of the
world, but the Spirit who is from God, that we might know the
things that have been freely given to us by God"
(1 Corinthians 2:12).

When you need to know what to do in a certain situation,

ask God for wisdom. God has promised to give wisdom to you "liberally and without reproach" when you ask for it (James 1:5). Liberally means openly and bountifully.[8] So, God will give you an abundance of wisdom whenever you ask. And He gives it "without reproach," meaning He won't criticize you or disapprove when you ask for it. God wants you to understand His will for your life.

Because the Holy Spirit lives inside you, God can give you direction by prompting you from within. As it says in Isaiah, "Your ears shall hear a word behind you, saying, 'This is the way, walk in it,' whenever you turn to the right hand or whenever you turn to the left" (Isaiah 30:21). God gives you direction internally. It is important to remember that any internal guidance you receive from God will *always* line up with the Bible. If you think God has told you something and it contradicts the Bible in any way, it is not from God.

You may be looking for God to give you a sign when you are making a decision. Sometimes God will give you that sign. When Gideon wanted confirmation from God, he "put a fleece of wool on the threshing floor" and said to God, "if there is dew on the fleece only, and it is dry on all the ground, then I shall know" that You will do as You said (Judges 6:37). When Gideon "rose early the next morning," God had confirmed it the way Gideon asked, and Gideon "wrung the dew out of the fleece, a bowlful of water" (Judges 6:38).

Then Gideon asked for another confirmation, saying, "Do not be angry with me, but let me speak just once more: Let me test I pray just once more with the fleece; let it now be dry only on the fleece, but on all the ground let there be dew" (Judges 6:39). In His graciousness, God gave Gideon a second confirmation. The Bible tells us, "And God did so that night.

It was dry on the fleece only, but there was dew on all the ground" (Judges 6:40).

Depending on the circumstances, God may give you an amazing sign (like He did for Gideon), leaving no doubt in your mind that a specific direction is from Him. But God doesn't usually lead with signs and wonders. Most of the time, God will quietly speak to you.

In the Bible, we see God speaking to His prophet, Elijah, when he was discouraged.

> And behold, the LORD passed by, and a great and strong wind tore into the mountains and broke the rocks in pieces before the LORD, but the LORD was not in the wind; and after the wind an earthquake, but the LORD was not in the earthquake; and after the earthquake a fire, but the LORD was not in the fire; and after the fire a still small voice. (1 Kings 19:11-12)

God spoke to Elijah in a still, small voice. And He often speaks to us in the same way. This truth is so important that it's worth repeating it—God speaks to us in a still, small voice. Stop waiting for the earthquake. Instead, make it a priority to spend time alone with God, quietly waiting on Him and listening for His voice.

When I have been praying about a decision I need to make, God will often speak to me by bringing to remembrance a verse

> " GOD SPEAKS TO US IN A STILL, SMALL VOICE. "

from the Bible that is relevant to the situation. It usually comes in a quiet moment when I am waiting on Him.

Spend time with God. Talk to Him but also give Him a

chance to speak to you. Remember, it's a conversation not a monologue. It's not one-sided where you go to Him and do all the talking. Take the time to hear from God. Your Creator wants to speak to you.

Protection

There is a spiritual realm that we usually cannot see. We get a glimpse into this realm through God's prophet, Elisha.

When Elisha and his servant were surrounded by a great army with horses and chariots, the servant was afraid (2 Kings 6:15). Elisha told his servant, "Do not fear, for those who are with us are more than those who are with them" (2 Kings 6:16). Elisha then prayed that God would open the servant's eyes so he could see (2 Kings 6:17). "Then the LORD opened the eyes of the young man, and he saw. And behold, the mountain was full of horses and chariots of fire all around Elisha" (2 Kings 6:17).

Both angels and demons reside in that spiritual realm. God created angels; angels are not human. One misconception is that when we die, we become angels who can eventually earn wings if we work hard enough.

In the classic Christmas movie, *It's a Wonderful Life*, one such angel, Clarence, is hoping that he will finally get his wings by helping George Bailey who has given up on life. At the end of the movie, we hear the familiar refrain, "Every time a bell rings, an angel gets his wings."[9] But humans don't become angels. In fact, the Bible tells us that, one day, we will judge angels (1 Corinthians 6:3). I don't know how that will work, but it's an interesting thought.

Angels are spiritual beings created by God to serve Him

(Psalm 104:4). They are exceedingly numerous (Revelation 5:11) and have been given great power (2 Kings 19:35). Angels can become visible in the semblance of human form (Genesis 19:1). The Bible reveals that there are angels that protect us (Psalm 91:10-11); guide us (Matthew 2:19-20); help us (Acts 12:7-11); intervene in our lives (Daniel 10:13); and escort those who believe in Jesus into heaven (Luke 16:22). The Bible even suggests that believers have guardian angels (Matthew 18:10).

At some point, the angel Lucifer (who is more commonly referred to as Satan or the devil) rebelled and rejected God's authority over him because he wanted to be like God (Isaiah 14:12-14). Jesus said that He "saw Satan fall like lightning from heaven" (Luke 10:18). Although God created him, Satan wrongfully wants to be worshipped rather than worshipping God, his Creator. Satan even tried to get Jesus to fall down and worship him (Matthew 4:9).

Satan hates humans. He leads a host of demons that help him do his work (Matthew 12:26-27). He has set out to keep us from enjoying a relationship with God. He began his work in the Garden of Eden when he appeared to Eve in the form of a serpent and tempted her by questioning God's authority and appealing to her pride (Genesis 3:1-5). Jesus warned us that Satan is a thief who "does not come except to steal, and to kill, and to destroy" (John 10:10). Because his mission is to destroy us, it is easy to fall into the trap of being afraid.

Fear can be a powerful thing. It manifests itself in two basic ways: either it will motivate you or paralyze you. The first type of fear is a catalyst that prompts you to do something. For example, the combination of procrastination and an impending deadline can cause a healthy fear to rise up. You become motivated by a desire to either maintain your reputation or avoid disappointing someone. That fear can encourage you to work harder to meet the deadline. But the other type of fear is unhealthy and debilitating. With that type of fear, you become frozen in your tracks, unable to move forward.

The Bible talks about these two types of fear. The first, the fear of the Lord, is a healthy fear that motivates us to please God, respect His commands, and do what is right. Among other things, the Bible teaches us the following:

- "The fear of the Lord is the beginning of wisdom; a good understanding have all those who do His commandments" (Psalm 111:10).
- "The fear of the Lord is the beginning of knowledge, but fools despise wisdom and instruction" (Proverbs 1:7).
- "The fear of the Lord is a fountain of life, to turn one away from the snares of death" (Proverbs 14:27).
- "[B]y the fear of the Lord one departs from evil" (Proverbs 16:6).

The Hebrew word for fear in each of those verses is iyr'a, which means respect, reverence, piety.[10] We should have a respect for God, holding Him in the highest regard.

God is due this respect based on who He is. King Darius recognized that we should fear God. After God delivered Daniel from the lions' den by sending an angel to shut the lions' mouths (Daniel 6:22), King Darius proclaimed:

He is the living God, and steadfast forever; His kingdom is the one which shall not be destroyed, and His dominion shall endure to the end. He delivers and rescues, and He works signs and wonders in heaven and on earth. . . . (Daniel 6:26-27).

In contrast, the Bible tells us about a second kind of fear—the fear of man or evil. This type of fear does not motivate us to do anything good. Instead, it often causes us to shut down and keeps us from doing what we should do. The enemy wants you to be afraid, to keep you paralyzed by fear. But God wants you to be free, trusting in Him. "For God has not given us a spirit of fear, but of power and of love and of a sound mind" (2 Timothy 1:7). The Greek word for fear in this verse means timidity and cowardice.[11] So we know that if we have that paralyzing kind of fear, it is not from God.

In many places in the Bible, we see God telling someone not to be afraid. Why? Because they were fearful.

When Moses spoke to the Israelites as they were getting ready to cross over the Jordan River into the land that God had promised them, he told them, "Be strong and of good courage, do not fear nor be afraid of them; for the LORD your God, He is the One who goes with you. He will not leave you nor forsake you" (Deuteronomy 31:6).

After Moses died and Joshua took his place in leading the Israelites, God reminded him,

Have I not commanded you? Be strong and of good courage; do not be afraid, nor be dismayed, for the LORD your God is with you wherever you go. (Joshua 1:9)

Just as God was with Joshua, He will be with His children. God promises throughout the Bible that He will be with and protect them. As God said in Isaiah, "Fear not, for I am with you; be not dismayed, for I am your God. I will strengthen you, yes, I will help you, I will uphold you with My righteous right hand" (Isaiah 41:10).

David acknowledged God's protection in his life. In Psalm 23:4, David declared, "Yea, though I walk through the valley of the shadow of death, I will fear no evil; for You are with me." And in Psalm 139:5, David said to God, "You have hedged me behind and before, and laid Your hand upon me."

> **THE CREATOR OF THE UNIVERSE IS HOLDING US IN HIS HAND.**

Under the new covenant, we also have God's protection. When you become a child of God, the Holy Spirit lives inside of you (John 14:16-17). You are sealed by the Holy Spirit (Ephesians 4:30). Satan knows that you belong to God and that he no longer has direct access to you.

As God's children, the Bible gives us a picture of being held in our good Shepherd's hand. Jesus said,

> And I give them eternal life, and they shall never perish; neither shall anyone snatch them out of My hand. My Father, who has given them to Me, is greater than all; and no one is able to snatch them out of My Father's hand. I and My Father are one. (John 10:28-30)

The Creator of the universe is holding us in His hand. It is so beautiful to know that Jesus is holding on to me. That means when I mess up, have a day when I'm feeling insecure, or forget to look to Him for something, I'll be okay because I'm in His hand. When I let go, He still has me firmly in His grasp.

My pastor has described it this way—it's like a parent walking with his small child across the street. To the child, it may seem as if he's holding the parent's hand. But if the child lets go or if danger arises, the parent has ahold of that child's hand to keep him safe and secure.

Because Jesus is holding on to us, we can be assured that "neither death nor life, nor angels nor principalities nor powers, nor things present nor things to come, nor height nor depth, nor any other created thing, shall be able to separate us from the love of God which is in Christ Jesus our Lord" (Romans 8:38-39).

As He holds on to us, Jesus intercedes on our behalf while He sits at the right hand of the Father (Romans 8:34). Jesus is praying for us. Even before Jesus died on the cross, the Bible tells us that Jesus interceded for His disciples. Jesus told Peter, "Satan has asked for you, that he may sift you as wheat. But I have prayed for you, that your faith should not fail" (Luke 22:31-32).

Soon thereafter, Jesus also interceded for us. During the Passover meal that Jesus shared with His disciples before He was arrested, Jesus prayed for His disciples (John 17:6-19). Then He prayed for us, saying,

> I do not pray for these alone [His disciples], but also for those who will believe in Me through their word; that they all may be one, as You, Father, are in Me, and I in You; that they also may be one in Us, that the world may believe that You sent Me. (John 17:20-21)

Isn't that amazing? We belong to Jesus, and He will

continue to intercede on our behalf. When you start to become fearful, remember that Jesus is praying for you.

The good Shepherd was faithful to lay down His life for you, and He will be faithful to protect you. In overcoming death, Jesus defeated Satan and his demons. All "angels and authorities and powers" are subject to Him (1 Peter 3:22). So, there is no reason for us to fear Satan. We know how everything will ultimately end—just read the book of Revelation. When you are afraid, remind yourself whose side you are on, because "He who is in you is greater than he who is in the world" (1 John 4:4).

Going Deeper

1. Journal about a way God has provided for you. Set it up as an Ebenezer stone so you will remember how God has provided for you in your life. Thank God and praise Him for His provision.

2. Train yourself to go to God for guidance when you have a decision to make. What do you need guidance for now?

Write down the decision you need to make and a prayer asking God for guidance and wisdom in making the decision. Wait on God to answer you.

3. Spiritual warfare is real. The Bible tells us, "For we do not wrestle against flesh and blood, but against principalities, against powers, against the rulers of the darkness of this age, against spiritual hosts of wickedness in the heavenly places" (Ephesians 6:12). God has given us a way to protect ourselves during spiritual warfare. He has given us spiritual armor. But we need to put it on every day. Read Ephesians 6:13-17. What are the six pieces of spiritual armor that God has given to protect us?

4. When you put on that armor, don't forget the next important step that the Bible tells us to do, "praying always with all prayer and supplication in the Spirit" (Ephesians 6:18). As you go through your day, you need to stay in constant contact with God. He is the One who fights the

battle on your behalf, and the One who will protect you. Write out a prayer asking God to help you fight the battles you are going through.

5. The sword of the Spirit is a powerful weapon. The Bible teaches us that the sword of the Spirit is "the word of God" (Ephesians 6:17). The Greek for "word" in that verse, rhema, means "that which is or has been uttered by the living voice."[12] It's the spoken word of God.

One way you can use this piece of spiritual armor is to resist temptations from the enemy. The Bible shows us that Jesus used the sword of the Spirit when Satan tempted Him after He had been fasting for 40 days and 40 nights in the desert (Matthew 4:1-2). Each time Satan tempted Him, Jesus referred to passages in the Old Testament, saying, "It is written" (Matthew 4:4, 7, 10).

For example, when Satan tempted Jesus by telling Him, "If You are the Son of God, command that these stones become bread" (Matthew 4:3), Jesus responded, "It is written, 'Man shall not live by bread alone, but by every word that proceeds from the mouth of God'" (Matthew 4:4 (quoting Deuteronomy 8:3)).

Memorize Bible verses so you can withstand the temptations of the enemy. In the moment of being tempted, you are unlikely to take the time to open your Bible. But if you have already committed them to memory, you will be able to effectively use the sword of the Spirit when temptations come your way.

Start by memorizing Ephesians 6:12 so you will remember that our spiritual battles must be fought with the spiritual tools God has given us. Write the verse on a 3x5 card and carry it with you so it is convenient to look at during your day. Before long, you will have that verse hidden in your heart, and you will be ready to use it when you need it.

5

YIELDING TO THE GOOD SHEPHERD

"THAT'S NOT PART OF MY PLAN."

That's what I thought when my husband told me about the possibility of him joining the staff at our church. You see, I had my own plan, and that plan did not involve my husband taking a job that would require a substantial pay cut.

Going on staff at our church would result in such a pay cut. Salaries at a church are typically lower than those paid at for profit companies or institutions since they are being paid out of the tithes and offerings given to the church. And going into the full-time ministry is itself an offering to the Lord. How would my plan come to fruition in that scenario? The cost of living was only increasing, and we were by no means independently wealthy.

Planning is not a bad thing. It's wise to plan. But our plans should always be subject to the Lord's plans for us. God has a plan for each one of us. He designed days for us before we were even born. The Bible tells us, "And in Your book they all were written, the days fashioned for me, when as yet there were none of them" (Psalm 139:16). Isn't that beautiful?

I had believed that my plan was based on a desire that the Lord had given me. God had given me the verse, "Delight yourself also in the LORD, and He shall give you the desires of your heart" (Psalm 37:4). Now, I know that the verse is not a "name it and claim it" type of thing. We don't get to use God as some sort of genie where we come up with stuff we want, ask Him for it, and expect it to come to fruition. Instead, the verse means that, as we delight ourselves in God (abide in Him), He plants the desires in our hearts. He gives us the desires themselves.

I really believed that God had planted a certain desire in my heart. It had been almost two years since I had received that desire. I prayed often for God to take the desire away if it was not from Him, to replace it with something else that was from Him, whatever that may be. But the desire had only grown. Based on that, I began to plan in the back of my mind what it would look like, how it would all come about.

God also gave me another verse—the one that follows the first one. "Commit your way to the LORD, trust also in Him, and He shall bring it to pass" (Psalm 37:5). I was doing what I could to ensure that I was completely committed to God. I had been getting rid of those things in my life that were either sinful or just not edifying and seeking Him and what He had for me and my husband.

And then there's the last part of that verse, "trust also in Him, and He shall bring it to pass" (Psalm 37:5). It was going to be God's work. *He* was going to bring it to pass, and not necessarily how I thought He would. The Bible tells us, "A man's heart plans his way, but the LORD directs his steps" (Proverbs 16:9).

I had to remember that God's ways are not our ways and His thoughts are not our thoughts. In fact, His ways are higher than our ways, and His thoughts are higher than our thoughts (Isaiah 55:8-9). And that's such a great thing. I am so thankful that God's ways and thoughts are not like mine. Mine are limited, sometimes jumbled, and not always wise and good.

Not only that, but God knows the beginning from the end (Isaiah 46:9-10), which means He knows everything. God can see how everything will work together and how something would be harmful to us if He allowed it. For this reason, we can trust that God knows the best way for each one of us. Simply put, His plan is *always* better.

"Yes Lord."

For those reasons, we should trust Him. As the Bible says, "Trust in the Lord with all your heart, and lean not on your own understanding; in all your ways acknowledge Him, and He shall direct your paths" (Proverbs 3:5-6). While meditating on these verses, I realized that it commands you to trust God with all your *heart*, not all your mind. God wants you to trust Him with your heart. It's not a process of thinking it through, reasoning so that you can figure out what the Lord is going to do or how and when He's going to do it. Instead, we are to trust Him.

In our lives, there are many things that we trust with our minds. We come to conclusions based on the knowledge we have

> " **GOD WANTS YOU TO TRUST HIM WITH YOUR HEART.** "

acquired and the experiences we have lived through. For example, I trust that when I sit on a chair it will hold me and not break if it is in good condition. I know from experience that chairs are usually built well. And if it is well-built, it feels sturdy. I can reason with my mind that the outcome will be okay (and even restful) if I sit down on a particular chair.

Likewise, if I am driving a new car, I know with my mind that it is unlikely to break down. I can reason that the parts have not yet worn out so the probability that it will fail is small. On the other hand, if the car has more than 100,000 miles on it, the likelihood of a part failing is much greater. Experience tells me that parts wear out with use and time.

But it's different when we're relying on God. He tells us to trust Him with our hearts. He is God, and we are not. Rather than trying to figure out what He is going to do when He has not yet revealed something to us, we should depend on Him. We should follow Him, believing that He will do what is best for us.

It's like when a father is leading a really young child by the hand. The child is not trying to figure out what her father is going to do or where they are going. Instead, the child happily follows her father, holding his hand as he leads her to where they are going. How much more can we trust our Father in heaven to lead us as we walk by His side.

And that trust is made easier when we remember that God is faithful. We know we can trust Him because His track record of faithfulness in our lives is 100%. We can spend time meditating on the Ebenezer stones in our lives—how God has already been faithful to lead and guide us. As Pastor Ed Taylor has said, "God's past faithfulness demands our present trust."[1]

Instead of trusting God with my heart, I had been leaning on my own understanding. It's what we're all inclined to do.

The Lord has been teaching me to trust Him, to walk by

faith and not by sight (2 Corinthians 5:7). I like to have everything laid out for me. I like to have a plan. You write down your goal, whatever it is that you want to accomplish, and then you plan how you are going to achieve it. Step-by-step. Do step one. Then do step two. Each step neatly laid out. Predictable.

But that's not how God works. Not with me anyway. I think it's because I'm still too self-reliant. He is teaching me to rely on Him for everything. So He gives me step one. And He doesn't give me step two until I've been obedient to complete the first step.

It's so hard to let go. I have to keep reminding myself that God knows exactly what is going to happen and how He is going to get me to where He wants me to go. He already knows each step and how He will perfectly orchestrate not just my steps but everything around me so that it will all work together to achieve exactly what He wants, what pleases Him.

And He *will* do all His pleasure (Isaiah 46:10). "Whatever the LORD pleases He does, in heaven and in earth" (Psalm 135:6).

I have to remind myself that I could never do what God does. I don't have that power. "He must increase, but I must decrease" (John 3:30).

I realized that I had been holding on to my plan—the way I wanted God to fulfill the desire that He had given me. But it wasn't for me to determine how to fulfill that desire. It was God's work, not mine. I had been praying, telling God that I was giving that desire to Him and asking Him to do with it what He pleased. Yet, when I looked down, I saw that my hands were tightly closed, still holding on to it, still wanting it to happen my way.

God showed me my hands and reminded me that I could not receive what He had for me until I opened my hands and let go of what was already in them (my plan). God never forces us to open our hands to Him. Instead, He patiently waits for us to fully come to Him on our own.

And then I felt fear, fear of letting it go, fear about what God wanted to do. What if I didn't like what God had for me? My heart was wrong. As the Bible tells us, "The heart is deceitful above all things, and desperately wicked; who can know it" (Jeremiah 17:9). God knows it; He knows me inside and out (Psalm 139:1). He even understands my thoughts (Psalm 139:2).

> " GOD IS FAITHFUL, EVERY MOMENT OF EVERY DAY. "

So I repented, "God forgive me for devising my own plan, for relying on that plan instead of trusting you. Forgive me for wanting what I want more than what You have for me." I reminded myself that I shouldn't be afraid. God is good. I looked back on my life and all of the amazing things He has done—so many things that I could not have done myself. God is faithful, every moment of every day.

And I remembered what my life was like when I did everything my way, when I made all of my own plans and executed those plans without God's help. I had been miserable and everything had seemed pointless. But when I started doing things God's way, I had peace, fulfillment, joy, love, and so much more.

Watching God do His work in His way is always so amazing. Why would this be any different? And so, I opened my tightly clenched fists and spread out my empty palms before Him, asking Him to give me whatever plan He had for me.

Do you have your own plan for your life that you've been holding on to? Have you tried to justify the fact that you're holding on to it? Are you trying to do your own thing, in your own way? God has a plan for your life. You won't be able to walk in the days He has planned for you until you let go of what you want to do. When you let go, you will be able to follow your good Shepherd, Jesus, as He leads and guides you.

After relenting to Him, I asked God what He wanted to do in our lives with my husband's job. My husband and I were independently seeking confirmation about what God wanted us to do. Did He want my husband to leave his current job and go on staff at our church? I asked God for a word. I prayed for a couple of days and didn't receive anything.

Then my husband told me that he had received a word. He had received direction from the Lord about what He wanted. But we decided that he would not share that word with me until I had received something. So I continued to pray.

On Sunday morning, I woke up and stayed in bed praying. I like to pray before I get up. It helps me to put my mind in the right perspective. A verse from Matthew came into my head, "seek first the kingdom of God and His righteousness, and all these things shall be added to you" (Matthew 6:33).

The verse seemed to address exactly where I was at. All the things that had been rolling through my head for the last several days were addressed by the verse. I had been thinking about things like, "If my husband's pay is cut, would we be able to still live in the house we had recently bought? Could we afford the mortgage along with all of our other living expenses? Even if we were able to eek by, would we ever be able to afford to go on a vacation? Would we be able to afford anything extra?" You know, the usual things a person would be concerned about when faced with a pay cut.

Later that day, my husband asked me if I had received a word. I told him that I thought I had but didn't have time to look up the verse and read it in context. And I wasn't sure that it was *the* word. I told him I would look up the verse and continue praying.

When I looked up the verse in context, I saw that it was speaking about the worries we have in life. It tells us not to worry about what we will eat, what we will drink, or the clothes we will wear. It tells us that God takes care of the birds, and we are of more value than those birds (Matthew 6:25-32). That portion of scripture then ends by telling us, "Therefore do not worry about tomorrow, for tomorrow will worry about its own things. Sufficient for the day is its own trouble" (Matthew 6:34).

I believed I had confirmation that my husband should work at our church if the Lord opened up that door. But I wanted to be sure.

On Monday morning, I prayed for confirmation that the word I had received the day before was truly from Him. I realize now that I was like Gideon, setting out a fleece before God. I listened to sermons on my way to work, but I didn't hear any further confirmation. I did my morning devotions before I started work. Nothing.

Then I prayed that God would confirm the exact verse I had received the day before. I prayed for God to give the verse to my husband—the same, exact one. I said, "God, I know that You are all-powerful, and if You wanted to give the same verse to my husband, You could." And I continued to look for confirmation throughout the day. I also listened to sermons on the way home. Nothing.

That night, my husband asked me if I had received a word. I told him that I thought I had but wanted him to tell me what his word was first. He said, "I received another word today. This one was very specific and it just popped into my head. And I kept thinking about it over and over." But he first told me about the one he had received on Friday. Then he told me the verse he had received that morning, "seek first the kingdom of God. . . ."

I started crying. After talking it through, I learned that he had received the verse while I was praying for God to give it to him. Out of over 31,000 verses in the Bible, what are the odds that my husband would think of the same, exact verse while I was praying for God to give it to him?

Our God is so amazing. I don't know why I'm surprised each time God does something like that, but I am. He confirmed, not only the verse that He had given me, but the fact that He cares about me enough that He was willing to give my husband the same, exact one.

So, the Lord did open the door for my husband to go on staff at our church. And, his pay was cut by more than half of what he had been earning. We held on to the verse in Matthew 6:33 that God had given to us. The verse is now on the wall in our dining room. And it seems to come up in various ways several times a month.

The Lord has provided in awesome ways since then, so much that I've told my husband numerous times that the math doesn't seem to make sense. God has given us an overflowing abundance in ways I would not have imagined. We have more left over at the end of each month now than we've ever had before. God has blessed us so much. It is truly evidence that where God guides, He also provides. As the Bible tells us, "God shall supply all your need according to His riches in glory by Christ Jesus" (Philippians 4:19). He is our great provider and our good Shepherd.

Going Deeper

1. Do you need to yield to the good Shepherd in any area of your life? Remember that you cannot walk in the days that He has fashioned for you while you are holding on to your own plans. Examine yourself and journal about any areas of your life that you need to surrender to God. If you're not sure if something is part of God's plans for you, ask God to show you.

2. Has God ever given you direction about a decision you had to make? Set up an Ebenezer stone by writing down the

occurrence so you will remember how God has guided you. Thank God and praise Him for speaking to you.

3. We have all had times when we leaned on our own understanding instead of trusting God with all our heart. Memorize Proverbs 3:5-6 so you will be able to remind yourself to trust in the Lord with all your heart the next time you are going through something. Begin by writing out the verses here.

6

DOING GOD'S WORK

WE ARE NOT SAVED BY DOING GOOD WORKS. RATHER, WE ARE saved by grace, through faith, for those good works (Ephesians 2:8-10). God chooses to do His work through the men and women who follow Him. Because He is all-powerful, God could accomplish His will—do His work—without us. But God gives us the privilege of being a part of what He is doing. He blesses us with the joy of doing His work. And He is faithful to help us do that work when we abide in Him.

Abiding in Jesus

We cannot do God's work on our own. Jesus told us that when we abide in Him, we can bear "much fruit" but without Him we "can do nothing" (John 15:5). Jesus explained, "Abide in Me, and I in you. As the branch cannot bear fruit of itself, unless it abides in the vine, neither can you, unless you abide in Me. I am the vine, you are the branches" (John 15:4-5).

A branch receives all of its nourishment from the vine that

it is attached to. If you remove the branch from the vine, it will dry up and die. It won't start growing grapes after it has been removed. In the same way, if we are removed from the true vine, Jesus, we won't be able to bear any fruit. That is, we won't be able to do God's work. To be fruitful (do His work), we must abide in Jesus.

What does it mean to abide in Jesus? The Greek word for abide is meno, which means to stay in a given state, to be present or remain.[1] And so, we are commanded to be present in Jesus, to remain in Jesus. How do we do that? Simply put, we abide in Jesus by spending time with Him.

Others can tell when we've been with Jesus. When the rulers, elders, and scribes "saw the boldness of Peter and John" in speaking God's word, they marveled. They knew that Peter and John had not been educated or trained. For that reason, "they realized that they had been with Jesus" (Acts 4:13). Just as they were able to tell that Peter and John had been with Jesus, people will know by watching us if we have been spending time with Him.

When we spend time with Jesus, our relationship with Him grows closer and more intimate. The type of relationship that you have with someone depends, in part, on how much time you spend with them.

Think about an acquaintance that you have. You may know her name, what she looks like, and some details about her life. You may know if she is married or has children. You may even know something she likes to do, if she works outside the home, or where she lives. But you don't know much else about her. You probably don't know what she dreams about or hopes for.

Now think about a close relationship. You know more than

a few details about her life. You know about the difficulties she has gone through and have encouraged her during those times. You know her dreams, likes and dislikes, personality, and how she views the world. And she knows you in the same way. Because you have shared aspects of your life together, your relationship has a warm, loving quality that you don't share with your acquaintances.

God doesn't want to be your acquaintance; He wants to have a close relationship with you. God already knows everything about you. He formed you in your mother's womb (Job 31:15; Psalm 139:13). He knows each trial you have gone through, every circumstance you've been in, and everything you have ever said or done. He sees everything (Proverbs 15:3). No one can hide from Him (Jeremiah 23:24). He even understands your thoughts and knows what you are going to say before you say it (Psalm 139:2, 4).

And, if you are born again, His Spirit lives inside you (John 14:16-17). He is with you wherever you go, every moment of every day. Even in those mundane moments of driving, shopping for groceries, cleaning, or cooking, He is with you.

But how much do you know about God? He has revealed Himself to us in the Bible. The Bible is His Word. It is inspired by the Holy Spirit and is "profitable for doctrine, for reproof, for correction, for instruction in righteousness, that the man of God may be complete, thoroughly equipped for every good work" (2 Timothy 3:16-17). In the Bible, God shares with us what He loves and what He hates. He tells us about many of the things He has done.

When you spend time reading the Bible, you get to know God more intimately, and He reveals Himself to you. As you read, the Holy Spirit helps you to understand (John 14:26) because He wants you to know Him. He wants you to be close to Him.

And how much time do you spend with God? Many people only think about God, read the Bible, and sing to God when they go to church on a weekend, to a mid-week service, or to a Bible study. Those things are good. We should have our focus on God during those times and continue "steadfastly in the apostles' doctrine and fellowship, in the breaking of bread, and in prayers" (Acts 2:42). But even if you did all three, that only accounts for about six hours out of your week. God has given each one of us 168 hours each week. If you only spent six hours a week with your husband, how close would you be to each other?

> **THE CREATOR OF THE UNIVERSE WANTS TO SPEND TIME WITH YOU.**

The point is not to count the hours you spend at church or in Bible study. A relationship doesn't grow by keeping track of the time we spend with the other person. For example, if you decided to spend one hour a day reading God's word and praying and then dutifully checked that hour off your to-do list because you felt like you had to do it, it is unlikely to bring you closer to Jesus. Because you are so intent on completing a task, you may not even remember what you read.

Instead, the proper perspective is to remember that we get to spend time with Jesus. The Creator of the universe wants to spend time with you. What if when we prayed, God said, "Oh no, it's her again." I praise God that He is not like that. The Bible tells us that He rejoices over us with singing (Zephaniah 3:17). He loves us! God's love for us is so great that He demonstrated that "love toward us, in that while we were still sinners,

Christ died for us" (Romans 5:8). When we love Jesus, we want to spend time with Him.

It reminds me of how some families have lives that revolve around a sport. For instance, I know parents who have a child who plays soccer. During soccer season, their lives are focused around soccer. There are practices and games many times during the week. Some of the games are in different parts of the metro area, requiring travel of one to three hours. They plan snacks and carpools. The process takes up the family's time, energy, and finances. The heart is the motivation for it all. It may be your child's desire because he loves the sport. Or it may be your desire to have him be part of something, to have the experience.

In a similar way, when you are following Jesus, your family's life should revolve around Jesus. The heart component is your desire to serve your Savior, to submit to your Lord, and to be with Him. It should take up your time and energy. It should consume your life. As David put it, "I have set the LORD always before me" (Psalm 16:8). David is a good role model, because we know that God called him a man after His own heart (Acts 13:22).

If you have children, you should teach them God's words, "speaking of them when you sit in your house, when you walk by the way, when you lie down, and when you rise up" (Deuteronomy 11:19). When you wake your children up in the morning, you can pray with them, asking God to watch over them during the day. When you're out for a walk and see a beautiful flower, you can tell your kids that God created that flower. There are so many ways you can make God part of your conversation throughout the day.

To be present with Jesus is to keep our thoughts continually on Him. We should view our entire lives through Jesus—considering what He wants us to do, what He wants us to say, what He wants us to think about, and where He wants us to go. It's like putting on a pair of sunglasses. The tinted lenses color everything you look at. Similarly, we are to "put on the Lord Jesus Christ" (Romans 13:14). We should view everything through the lens of the Bible. When we do, we will make decisions based on what God wants us to do.

The Bible tells us that we should "pray without ceasing" (1 Thessalonians 5:17). Prayer is simply talking to God. You don't have to get down on your knees, fold your hands, and close your eyes to pray. Not that it is wrong to do so. But you can pray while you're making dinner or when you're driving your car. You can pray anywhere, anytime of the day. You can pray by thinking in your head or speaking the prayer out loud.

If you remind yourself that God is with you wherever you are, you can talk to Him throughout your day. Thank Him that you were able to pay for the gas in your car or buy groceries. Ask Him for wisdom about what you should do when you have a decision to make. Praise Him for a friend that you get to have dinner with. If we draw near to God by thinking about Him and talking to Him, He has promised to draw near to us (James 4:8).

In the Bible, we see that Mary knew what it means to abide in Jesus. She "sat at Jesus' feet and heard His word" (Luke 10:39). When her sister Martha complained that Mary wasn't helping her, Jesus commended Mary, saying, "But one thing is needed, and Mary has chosen that good part, which will not be taken away from her" (Luke 10:42).

Like Mary, we need to spend time sitting at Jesus' feet, hearing His word. We need to read the Bible and hear His voice. We need to sit and listen. God tells us, "Be still, and know that I am God" (Psalm 46:10). It's that time in His word that leads to further meditation on His word, then to acting on what we hear by being "doers of the word" (James 1:22). That's what keeps us abiding in Him. When we do those things, we are like the blessed man whose "delight is in the law of the Lord," meditating on God's word "day and night" (Psalm 1:2).

Power to Do God's Work

As we abide in Jesus, God empowers us to do His work. Jesus promised that God the Father would give us the Holy Spirit to help us. Jesus said,

> If you love Me, keep My commandments. And I will pray the Father, and He will give you another Helper, that He may abide with you forever—the Spirit of truth, whom the world cannot receive, because it neither sees Him nor knows Him; but you know Him, for He dwells with you and will be in you. (John 14:15-17)

The Holy Spirit gives us power to be witnesses for Jesus wherever God sends us (Acts 1:8). The same Holy Spirit that raised Jesus from the dead lives in the believer (Romans 8:11).

We see an example of how the Holy Spirit helps us do God's work in the life of Peter. The Bible shows us a stark difference between Peter without the Holy Spirit and Peter with the Holy Spirit. After Jesus was taken into custody, Peter denied Jesus three times (twice to two different servant girls) because he was afraid (Matthew 26:69-75). Later on, Jesus rose from the dead and ascended into Heaven (Luke 24:1-7; Acts 1:9).

Jesus had told the disciples to wait in Jerusalem "until you are endued with power from on high" (Luke 24:49). The disciples did as Jesus commanded (Acts 1:4-5, 2:1). Then the Holy Spirit came as Jesus promised (Acts 2:2-4). When the Holy Spirit came upon Peter, he boldly preached that Jesus is the risen Messiah when the people mocked them (Acts 2:13-40). God empowered Peter with His Spirit to speak the words He wanted the people to hear. As a result, 3,000 people were saved (Acts 2:41).

> **❝ WHO GOD IS, IS MORE IMPORTANT THAN WHO YOU ARE. ❞**

And God still empowers His followers to do whatever He has called them to do. Jesus promised that God the Father will give the Holy Spirit to those who ask Him (Luke 11:13). When God prompts you to do something—like share the gospel with someone or invite somebody to church—if you ask God to help you, He will.

Part of that power comes from remembering that God is with us when we do His work. As Jesus said, "I am with you always, even to the end of the age" (Matthew 28:20). If God sends you, He will be with you. Who God is, is more important than who you are.

As you do His work, remember not to do it in your own strength. As God told Zerubbabel about his work in rebuilding the temple, "Not by might nor by power, but by My Spirit" (Zechariah 4:6). It can be tempting to do something God has asked you to do without praying, without seeking His help. That is always a mistake. Remember that Jesus told us that we can do nothing without Him. We must abide in Jesus, asking for power from the Holy Spirit.

God Prepares the Way

Not only does God empower you to do the work, He has already orchestrated all of the circumstances surrounding what He wants you to do. We see an example of this in Luke 19:30-35. Jesus sent two of His disciples into a village to get a young donkey. Jesus instructed them,

> Go into the village opposite you, where as you enter you will find a colt tied, on which no one has ever sat. Loose it and bring it here. And if anyone asks you, "Why are you loosing it?" thus you shall say to him, "Because the Lord has need of it." (Luke 19:30-31)

When the disciples went into the village, they found the colt "just as [Jesus] had said to them" (Luke 19:32). While they were untying the colt to take it back to Jesus, the colt's owners asked them what they were doing (Luke 19:33). The disciples answered with the words Jesus had told them to say and then took the colt to Jesus (Luke 19:34-35).

Before the disciples went to get the colt, God had already prepared the way before them. If God hadn't done so, the colt's owners likely would have protested in some way or had them arrested for stealing. Instead, everything went just as Jesus had told them it would go.

So, we should respond with immediate obedience when God tells us to do something. We see examples in the Bible of people who immediately obeyed when God called them. As a result, they were blessed with the privilege of being a part of God's work.

When God told Abraham (then still called Abram) to "[g]et out of your country, from your family and from your father's house, to a land that I will show you," the Bible tells us that he "departed as the LORD had spoken to him" (Genesis 12:1, 4). God didn't even tell Abraham where he was going. Yet, Abraham responded with obedience. Like Abraham, when Jesus called Peter and Andrew, they "immediately" left what they were doing and followed Him (Mark 1:16-18).

We should follow the examples given to us by Abraham and the apostles. Don't worry about whether you think you have the ability to do what God has called you to do. "God is not looking for ability as much as availability."[2] Remember that you can't do God's work in your own strength. God will equip you as you step out in obedience.

God Prepares You

God equips us to do His work by giving us spiritual gifts. There are gifts given to each person in various combinations, depending on what God has planned for you. But each person is given at least one spiritual gift. As Paul taught us,

> For as we have many members in one body, but all the members do not have the same function, so we, being many, are one body in Christ, and individually members of one another. Having then gifts differing according to the grace that is given to us, let us use them: if prophecy, let us prophesy in proportion to our faith; or ministry, let us use it in our ministering; he who teaches, in teaching; he who

exhorts, in exhortation; he who gives, with liberality; he who leads, with diligence; he who shows mercy, with cheerfulness. (Romans 12:4-8)

Jesus calls you into the ministry that He wants you to be in (1 Timothy 1:12). It's a calling. And He gives you spiritual gifts in accordance with the work He's called you to do. Those "gifts and the calling of God are irrevocable" (Romans 11:29).

Because we are all different, you shouldn't compare yourself to others as you do God's work. The Bible tells us that comparing

JESUS CALLS YOU INTO THE MINISTRY.

yourself with others is not wise (2 Corinthians 10:12). God has given each of us a race to run (Hebrews 12:1). And each one of our races is different.

Instead of focusing on what others are doing, you should focus on the work that God has given you. God prepared that work for you; you were created for it. "For we are His workmanship, created in Christ Jesus for good works, which God prepared beforehand that we should walk in them" (Ephesians 2:10).

As you step out in faith to do God's work, He will assist you as you move forward. It's like learning to ride a bicycle. When I was first learning, my dad put an extra set of wheels on my bike that extended off the back wheel to give it more stability. With the training wheels on, I could sit on the bike without balancing and get used to pedaling and moving forward without worrying about falling over.

After I got used to riding my bike with the training wheels, the day came when he took them off. Instead of the extra wheels, my dad held on to the back of the bike's seat, giving me a little more stability as I learned to balance. Before long, I had learned how to balance and could ride my bike without thinking about it. It had become second nature to me.

In a similar way, when God calls us to do His work, He doesn't push us into it when we're not ready. God is gracious to us. Like the training wheels on my bike, He helps us to get used to whatever He's called us to do before we go solo. The methods God uses will vary in each one of our lives. We are all different, and God tailors the help He gives us to our unique personalities and abilities.

We see an example of God's use of training wheels in the life of Moses. When God called Moses to lead the Israelites out of their slavery in Egypt, Moses wasn't quick to agree. Instead, he came up with several excuses about why he should not be the one to lead them.

Moses said to God, "Who am I that I should go to Pharaoh, and that I should bring the children of Israel out of Egypt?" (Exodus 3:11). In response, God told Moses that He would be with him and gave Moses a sign that He had sent him (Exodus 3:12).

Even with God's assurance, Moses still didn't agree to go, saying, "But suppose they will not believe me or listen to my voice; suppose they say, 'The LORD has not appeared to you'" (Exodus 4:1). God then gave Moses three miraculous signs to do before the Israelites so they would believe him (Exodus 4:2-9).

Yet, Moses came up with a third excuse. Moses said, "O my Lord, I am not eloquent, neither before nor since You have spoken to Your servant; but I am slow of speech and slow of tongue" (Exodus 4:10). "So the LORD said to him, 'Who has made man's mouth? Or who makes the mute, the deaf, the

seeing, or the blind? Have not I, the LORD?'" (Exodus 4:11).
God then told Moses that He would be with his mouth and
teach him what to say (Exodus 4:12).

Still, instead of submitting in obedience, Moses told God,
"O my Lord, please send by the hand of whomever else You
may send" (Exodus 4:13). In other words, "Thank you very
much, but please send someone else. I don't want to do it."

God, being so gracious to Moses, then tells Moses that his
brother Aaron, who could "speak well," could be his
spokesman (Exodus 4:14-16). God instructed Moses, "Now
you shall speak to him and put the words in his mouth. And I
will be with your mouth and with his mouth, and I will teach
you what you shall do" (Exodus 4:15).

Finally, Moses obeyed God. As we read, we see the
progression as Moses gets comfortable doing the work that
God called him to do.

Moses begins by relying on the "training wheels" that God
gave him. When Moses met Aaron, he told Aaron "all the
words of the LORD who had sent him, and all the signs which
He had commanded him" (Exodus 4:28). Moses and Aaron
gathered together the elders of the children of Israel, and
Aaron spoke "all the words which the LORD had spoken to
Moses" and did the signs in their sight (Exodus 4:29-30). "So
the people believed" (Exodus 4:31).

Later, Moses and Aaron went to Pharaoh, and *they* told
Pharaoh what God had told them to say (Exodus 5:1, 3).

Soon, we see Moses himself speaking to the Israelites and
to Pharaoh (Exodus 6:9; 8:9, 26).

Despite this rocky start, Moses made it into the revered
"Hall of Faith" and is remembered for the work that God did
through him. "By faith [Moses] forsook Egypt, not fearing the

wrath of the king; for he endured as seeing Him who is invisible" (Hebrews 11:27).

Just as God helped Moses, He will give you the "training wheels" you need to get started when you obediently step out in faith to do what He has called you to do. So when God gives you direction, step out in faith. Many times, God will not give you the next step or tell you where you are going until after you obey and take that first step.

Don't Hide Your Talent

Several years ago, I felt that God was calling me to write something. I wasn't sure what He wanted me to write. And I didn't take the time to ask Him. I didn't ask God for guidance because I was afraid. Afraid that I would write something that wouldn't glorify God. Afraid that I would get something wrong, especially if I wrote about the things of God. There is a stricter judgment for those who teach God's word. As James warned, "My brethren, let not many of you become teachers, knowing that we shall receive a stricter judgment" (James 3:1). Teachers must "rightly divid[e] the word of truth" (2 Timothy 2:15).

Then God showed me the parable of the talents. A talent was a unit of measurement used to weigh a coin. The amount of money represented by a talent varied in different places and times based on the laws regulating currency.[3] Likely, at the time Jesus taught this parable, a talent would have been equal to a year's wage.[4]

In the parable, a man who was going to travel to a "far country" gives his servants different amounts of talents according to each one's ability (Matthew 25:14-15). The man gave one servant five talents, another two talents, and another one talent (Matthew 25:15).

While their master was away, the servants with five and two talents each traded them and doubled the money (Matthew 25:16-17). "But he who had received one went and dug in the ground, and hid his lord's money" (Matthew 25:18).

When their master returned, the servants who had been given five and two talents, told their master how they had doubled what he had given them (Matthew 25:19-20, 22). In response, their master told each one, "Well done, good and faithful servant; you were faithful over a few things, I will make you ruler over many things. Enter into the joy of your lord" (Matthew 25:21, 23).

The servant who had received one talent told his master, "Lord, I knew you to be a hard man, reaping where you have not sown, and gathering where you have not scattered seed. And I was afraid, and went and hid your talent in the ground. Look, there you have what is yours" (Matthew 25:24-25).

His master responded,

> You wicked and lazy servant, you knew that I reap where I have not sown, and gather where I have not scattered seed. So you ought to have deposited my money with the bankers, and at my coming I would have received back my own with interest. So take the talent from him, and give it to him who has ten talents.
>
> For to everyone who has, more will be given, and he will have abundance; but from him who does not have, even what he has will be taken away. (Matthew 25:26-29)

Just as the master in the parable gave talents to his servants to invest for him while he was away, Jesus has given each of us talents to use for His glory while He is away preparing a place for us. When we refuse to use them for any reason or are lazy, we sin. God showed me that I was like the servant who hid the talent in the ground. I had not been using what God had given me for His glory.

> **66 JESUS HAS GIVEN EACH OF US TALENTS TO USE FOR HIS GLORY WHILE HE IS AWAY. 99**

God doesn't expect perfection from us. Sure, if we intentionally mislead people or spread false doctrine, that would be a different story. But God wants us to use the talents He has given us. He gave them to us for a reason. If just one person is encouraged or decides to follow Jesus, then it is worth it. I don't know about you, but I want to hear Jesus tell me one day, "Well done, good and faithful servant. Enter into the joy of your Lord."

Being Doers of the Word

I can recall many times when God has prompted me to do something or say something. There have been times when I have not been obedient, when I've been afraid to speak up. We need to remember in those times that we must fear God and not man because the "fear of man brings a snare, but whoever trusts in the LORD shall be safe" (Proverbs 29:25).

We also should remember that our days are limited, so we should take advantage of every opportunity to do God's work. As the psalmist said, "teach us to number our days, that we may gain a heart of wisdom" (Psalm 90:12).

Whenever I am obedient, it is amazing to see how God

works through me. I never regret doing something that He asks me to do.

On one such occasion, my husband and I were going on vacation a little more than a week before Christmas. We were staying at a hotel the night before our flight left. We had checked in at the front desk, making polite conversation with the woman who was working there that evening.

When we went up to our room, I felt God prompting me to take an invitation for our church's Christmas Eve services to the woman at the front desk. Bottom line, I didn't want to. We were getting settled, and I was ready to relax. After all, we were officially on vacation now. I began thinking about how awkward it would be to take her the invitation.

In the end, I obeyed. I prayed that God would help me. Then I went downstairs, invitation in hand. When I got to the front desk, I invited her to our church and handed her the invitation. As we began talking, I found out that she was also a believer in Jesus. Then she began telling me about her year. Her son had been murdered a few months before, and she had been diagnosed with breast cancer. She told me that she had been having a hard time that day. God knew she needed someone to pray with her, someone to encourage her. I had the privilege of being the person He used to do that.

You never know what God is going to do when He prompts you to do something like that. For all I knew, He just wanted to make sure she was invited to a church service where she would hear about His love for her. But in this case, one of His children needed someone to stand with her for a few moments. The Bible tells us, "Rejoice with those who rejoice, and weep with those who weep" (Romans 12:15). We are to "[b]ear one another's burdens" (Galatians 6:2).

So, the next time God prompts you to do something, step out in faith in obedience and see what He will do. Who knows whether God brought you to that place "for such a time as this?" (Esther 4:14).

Going Deeper

1. Do you know what God is calling you to do?

If so, what is it? If not, ask God. He will show you what He has for you. Does your church need someone to help in the children's ministry? Or someone to greet others before services? Or maybe they need help picking up trash so the grounds are more welcoming to people who are coming for the first time?

Pray about the needs of your church and ask God what He wants you to do. If you think you want to try something or think God has given you direction, step out in faith. God will help you as you do. Write out a prayer asking God to show you what He wants you to do.

2. Take time to examine yourself. Are you consistently abiding in Jesus? What are some of the ways that you abide in Him? How often do you spend time with Him? Journal about what your relationship with Jesus is like and ask God to help you draw closer to Him.

3. Journal about a way that God has worked through you. What did He ask you to do? Did you obey? What was the outcome?

7

WALKING BY FAITH WITH GOD

THE BIBLE INSTRUCTS US TO "WALK BY FAITH, NOT BY SIGHT" (2 Corinthians 5:7). As we go through life, we aren't always able to see what is ahead of us. We don't know with certainty what will happen tomorrow (or even later today for that matter). Even our best laid plans, seemingly set in concrete are sometimes disrupted. "We can make our plans, but the LORD determines our steps" (Proverbs 16:9 (NLT)). In other words, our steps are "ordered by the LORD" (Psalm 37:23). That's why we "ought to say, 'If the Lord wills, we shall live and do this or that'" (James 4:15).

Not only do we not know what will happen, sometimes the only thing we can see is the situation in front of us. Our limited vision causes us to be afraid; we aren't able to understand how things could ever get better.

Although we can't predict what will happen tomorrow, God knows all things (1 John 3:20). "His understanding is infinite" (Psalm 147:5). God knows everything that will happen in our lives. We can rely on God in every circumstance because

He already knows exactly what will happen as we go through our day. He is not surprised by anything.

And, God is powerful and in control. "God reigns over the nations" and "sits on His holy throne" (Psalm 47:8). As an illustration of God's sovereignty, the Bible tells us that God

> has made the earth by His power; He has established the world by His wisdom, and stretched out the heaven by His understanding. When He utters His voice—there is a multitude of waters in the heavens: He causes the vapors to ascend from the ends of the earth; He makes lightnings for the rain; He brings the wind out of His treasuries. (Jeremiah 51:15-16)

God "does great things, and unsearchable, marvelous things without number" (Job 5:9). As He told Jeremiah, "Behold I am the LORD, the God of all flesh. Is there anything too hard for me?" (Jeremiah 32:27).

"GOD IS POWERFUL AND IN CONTROL." The One who created you is able to help you through anything you may encounter. Walking *by faith* means that you trust God as you go through your day, knowing that He will be with you. By faith, you don't have to worry about the outcome of any situation because you know that God is in control. He is able to handle anything that may come your way.

In Hebrews 11, we see many illustrations of men and women who walked by faith with God. As you read through them, you might think that they must have been exceptional to do the things they did. You might tell yourself that you could never be like them. But if you read about the details of their lives in the Old Testament, you will see that they were people just like you and me. They are respected, not because they were perfect or had some sort of super powers, but because they lived lives of faith.

One of my favorite examples is Sarah. The Bible tells us, "By faith, Sarah herself also received strength to conceive seed, and she bore a child when she was past the age, because she judged Him faithful who had promised" (Hebrews 11:11). When we go back to the Old Testament, we learn that God made a promise to Sarah's husband, Abraham, that he would have an heir who would come from his own body and that his descendants would be as numerous as the stars (Genesis 15:4-5). At the time, Abraham and Sarah didn't have any children (Genesis 15:2-3).

We know Sarah had a lapse of faith about this promise because she persuaded Abraham to have a child with her maidservant, Hagar, so that Hagar's child could be Abraham's heir (Genesis 16:1-2). Although this practice was perfectly acceptable in that society, it was not what God had promised. Nevertheless, Abraham did as Sarah had suggested, and Hagar bore him a son named Ishmael (Genesis 16:2-4, 11).

Despite them taking matters into their own hands, God later reaffirmed this promise to Abraham when he was 99 years old and Sarah was 89, specifying that he would have a son by Sarah (Genesis 17:1, 4-6, 15-17). And when the Lord appeared to Abraham and told him that Sarah would have a son "according to the time of life," Sarah (who had been eavesdropping on their conversation in her tent) laughed within herself because she "had passed the age of childbearing" (Genesis 18:1, 10-12).

God called Sarah out on her laughter; He knew what she

was thinking. He asked Abraham, "Why did Sarah laugh?" (Genesis 18:13).

Yet, we know that she had faith because she did have a son, who they named Isaac, which means laughter[1] (Genesis 21:1-3). And we are told that it was by faith that she "received strength to conceive seed" (Hebrews 11:11). Perhaps it was God's reminder that built up her faith. In response to her laughter, God had asked (rhetorically, of course), "Is anything too hard for the LORD?" (Genesis 18:14).

What a remarkable example of faith, judging God faithful to give you a baby when you are 90 years old. We have to remember that God is all-powerful; He is able to do what He has promised. He is able to do things that would never be possible for us to do on our own. We need to believe that God is who He says He is. As it tells us in Hebrews 11:6, "without faith it is impossible to please Him, for he who comes to God must believe that He is, and that He is a rewarder of those who diligently seek Him."

It helps us to walk by faith and not by what we see when we meditate on God's promises. The Bible tells us about those promises. Many of them were specifically made to the Israelites. For example, God made promises about how He would deliver the Israelites from their bondage in Egypt and bring them into the promised land. We can read about those promises in the Old Testament and then see how God fulfilled them. In fact, "[n]ot a word failed of any good thing which the LORD had spoken to the house of Israel. All came to pass" (Joshua 21:45). Not part, but *all* of those promises came to pass.

God has also made promises to His children. And He is faithful to fulfill each one. Just as God fulfilled His promises to the Israelites, He will continue to be faithful to fulfill the promises He has made to us. God's past faithfulness means we can know He will fulfill His future promises.

When Jesus told His disciples that they were going to "cross over to the other side of the lake," (Luke 8:22) it was a promise to them that they would

> **GOD'S PAST FAITHFULNESS MEANS WE CAN KNOW HE WILL FULFILL HIS FUTURE PROMISES.**

make it to the other side. As they sailed, Jesus fell asleep (Luke 8:23). After he did, "a wind storm came down on the lake" and the boat was filling with water (Luke 8:23).

Jesus and His disciples were sailing across Lake Gennesaret, also called the Sea of Galilee or the Sea of Tiberius. The location of the lake and the shape of the hills surrounding it makes the sea "prone to sudden violent storms."[2]

Because the boat was filling with water, they were "in jeopardy" (Luke 8:23). So the disciples go and wake up Jesus, saying, "Master, Master, we are perishing!" (Luke 8:24). We would say, "We're going to die!"

We know that four of the disciples (James, John, Andrew, and Peter) were professional fisherman, and they were partners in the fishing business (Matthew 4:18-22; Mark 1:16-20; Luke 5:10). When Jesus called them to follow Him, they were working by Lake Gennesaret (Matthew 4:18; Luke 5:1). They had a lot of experience being in a boat on that very lake. If they were afraid of dying, the storm must have been really bad.

Jesus got up and rebuked the wind and the waves, which obeyed Him, and "there was a calm" (Luke 8:24). Then Jesus rebuked the disciples. He asked them, "Where is your faith?" (Luke 8:25).

Why would Jesus reprimand them when the storm had been so intense? Because He had told them that they were going to cross over to the other side. He didn't say they were going to *try* to cross over. Instead, He told them that they were going to do it.

When Jesus says that something is going to happen, we can trust Him. We can know that it will come to pass. If Jesus says to you, "Let us cross over to the other side of the lake," (Luke 8:22) you can know for certain that you will make it to the other side. You won't die before you make it there no matter how bad the storm. He will take you there. And He will be with you the entire time.

That's how God works. He doesn't make promises that He doesn't keep. As we saw earlier, God is faithful even when we are faithless (2 Timothy 2:13). So, when you read in the Bible about a promise that God has made, you can be sure that it will happen. And there are many, beautiful promises that God has made.

Every year, the Jewish people celebrate the Passover. During that feast, they recount how God freed the Israelites from slavery in Egypt. In modern times, they traditionally sing a song called Dayenu. Dayenu is a Hebrew word that means "it would have been sufficient." As a part of that song, someone recites a number of things that God did for the Israelites, starting with God bringing them out of Egypt, judging the Egyptians, and judging the Egyptian's idols.

After saying, if God had just brought them out of Egypt but not judged the Egyptians, all the people shout, "Dayenu!" That is, it would have been sufficient. It continues by saying, if

God had judged the Egyptians but not judged the Egyptians' idols, it would have been sufficient. The recitation continues through many things that God did for them, including dividing the Red Sea, giving them the Torah (the first five books of the Bible), providing for them in the desert for 40 years, bringing them into the land of Israel, and building the Holy Temple.[3]

God's promises to His children are like that. If God had just made a way for us to have our sins forgiven so that we

> **" GOD GIVES US PROMISES THAT WE CAN RELY ON. "**

would have eternal life, it would have been sufficient. But God did so much more. He wants to have a relationship with us. And, in His graciousness, God gives us promises that we can rely on and look forward to.

As we look at just a few of those promises, let us "stand in awe of Him. For He spoke, and it was done; He commanded, and it stood fast" (Psalm 33:8-9).

You are a New Creation in Christ

> Therefore, if anyone is in Christ, he is a new creation; old things have passed away; behold, all things have become new. (2 Corinthians 5:17)

The day you decided to follow Jesus, you became a new creation. By being born again, you are "in Christ." As the New Living Translation puts it, "This means that anyone who belongs to Christ has become a new person. The old life is gone; a new life has begun!" (2 Corinthians 5:17). Things you used to like, you now hate. And those things that you used to hate, you now love.

The sin you used to practice didn't bother you before. It was only after you were born again that you had a desire to stop doing those things. Before, curse words may have been a regular part of your vocabulary that you freely used. But now, you cringe when one accidentally slips out of your mouth.

The apostle Paul taught us that "[n]either fornicators, nor idolaters, nor adulterers, nor homosexuals, nor sodomites, nor thieves, nor covetous, nor drunkards, nor revilers, nor extortioners will inherit the kingdom of God. And such were some of you" (1 Corinthians 6:9-11). Did you catch that? And such *were* some of you. Practicing those sins is now a part of your past. It's part of the old things that have passed away. As Paul goes on to explain, "But you were washed, but you were sanctified, but you were justified in the name of the Lord Jesus and by the Spirit of our God" (1 Corinthians 6:11).

On the other hand, before you were born again, you didn't have a desire to read the Bible. You weren't interested in finding out what God had revealed to us. But since you were born again, you want to know the things that God loves and the things that God hates. You want to please Him. You want to worship Him. Because you are a new creation, God has given you new desires. You no longer have to identify with the person you once were.

Praise God for this promise. Even when you don't feel like you are a new creation, by faith, you can remind yourself that your old life is gone. God has given you a new one.

WALKING BY FAITH WITH GOD | 103

God Will Be with You

> For He Himself has said, "I will never leave you nor forsake
> you." (Hebrews 13:5 (quoting Deuteronomy 31:6))

As His child, God has promised that He will never leave you
or forsake you. Forsake means to abandon or desert; leave
helpless.[4]

The next time you feel alone, remind yourself that God is
with you. When you become a child of God, His Spirit lives
inside you (Galatians 2:20). He will not abandon you; He will
not leave you helpless. No matter where you are or what you
are doing, God is there. He is with you all the time.

It is especially important to remember this promise when
you are going through a trial. Those times when things are
dark and you feel like you can't take the next step, He is there.
You never have to be alone.

We don't always tangibly feel God's presence but, by faith,
we can hold on to this promise, knowing that it's true. You will
have trials, but Jesus will be with you through each one. And
He will be faithful to get you to the other side.

God is Working All Things Together for Good

> And we know that all things work together for good to those
> who love God, to those who are the called according to His
> purpose. (Romans 8:28)

God has promised that He is working all things together for
good. Do you know what the word "all" means in the Greek

language this verse was originally written in? It means just that—all, everything, the whole.[5] That means that God will somehow work together for good even the worst thing that has happened in your life. To clarify, it doesn't mean that the event itself was good. It just means that God can work whatever happened together for good. What an amazing promise.

The ultimate example of God working something together for good was Jesus' death on the cross. The Son of God was brutally beaten and then hung on a Roman cross to die. Before, during, and even right after Jesus' crucifixion, the disciples did not (and probably could not) understand the reason Jesus died.

Jesus had foretold His death to the disciples, saying, "The Son of Man is being betrayed into the hands of men, and they will kill Him. And after He is killed, He will rise the third day" (Mark 9:31). But the disciples "did not understand this saying, and were afraid to ask Him" (Mark 9:32). And when Jesus was taken into custody, "all the disciples forsook Him and fled" (Matthew 26:56).

After Jesus was resurrected and Peter saw the empty tomb, he "marvel[ed] to himself at what had happened" (Luke 24:12). The word marvel means to wonder.[6] Peter was thinking about it, wondering about what he saw. But he didn't yet understand. And even when Jesus first appeared to the eleven disciples, "they were terrified and frightened, and supposed they had seen a spirit" (Luke 24:37). It was only after Jesus told them to touch Him, ate in their presence, and "opened their understanding," that they finally got it (Luke 24:39-45).

The furthest thing from the disciples' minds was that God would use Jesus' death for good. But later, they understood.

Jesus had died for their sins and for the sins of all who would believe. They were forgiven and could have a relationship with God. God was able to use the most horrific tragedy—the death of His own Son—to save mankind.

Like the disciples, we probably can't see how God will take something bad that has happened in our lives and work it together for good. Our limited perspective keeps us from being able to see the big picture. Even after we have gone through a trial, we don't always understand why we went through it. Sometimes we get a glimpse of how God is using the trial; other times it seems there is no way anything good could come out of it.

But we can remember that God will be faithful to fulfill this promise. We can know, without seeing, that God will somehow use it for good. "For our light affliction, which is but for a moment, is working for us a far more exceeding and eternal weight of glory, while we do not look at the things which are seen, but at the things which are not seen" (2 Corinthians 4:17-18). By faith, we can count on God's promise that He will work all things together for good instead of being consumed by the whys of the trial.

You Will Live with Jesus

In My Father's house are many mansions; if it were not so, I would have told you. I go to prepare a place for you. And if I go and prepare a place for you, I will come again and receive you to Myself; that where I am, there you may be also. (John 14:2-3)

Jesus told His disciples about this promise right after they had shared their last Passover dinner together. It was the night Jesus was arrested. The following day, Jesus would be crucified on the cross for our sins.

Jesus had told the disciples that He would be going away, and they wouldn't be able to follow Him (John 13:33, 36). The disciples were troubled by the news that Jesus would be leaving them. We know that they were worried because Jesus told them, "Let not your heart be troubled" (John 14:1). It was in response to their worry that Jesus made this promise.

> **❝ ONE DAY, WE WILL SEE JESUS. ❞**

And the promise extends to us as well. We can't physically be with Jesus right now, but we can know that someday we will live with Him. He is preparing a place for us. When it is time, Jesus will receive us to Himself. One day, we will see Jesus. We will walk with Him and talk with Him. We will get to be with Him forever.

Praise God that one day we will be with Him. We can look forward to that promise, knowing that one day we will live with our good, good Father.

God Will Give You Eternal Life

> For the wages of sin is death, but the gift of God is eternal life in Christ Jesus our Lord. (Romans 6:23)

The word eternal means "without end, never to cease, everlasting."[7] I know the meaning of the word is obvious but let it sink in. Meditate on this promise. As God's children, we will have eternal life. Your body will die, but your spirit won't be condemned. Your life will never cease. It will continue without end.

Jesus Himself made us this promise. Jesus said, "For God so loved the world that He gave His only begotten Son, that whoever believes in Him should not perish but have everlasting life" (John 3:16). Although translated in this verse as "everlasting," the Greek word is the same one.

So, what will living that eternal life be like? The Bible tells us that we will understand things in a way that we never could now. As Paul told us, "For now we see in a mirror, dimly, but then face to face. Now I know in part, but then I shall know just as I also am known" (1 Corinthians 13:12). There are trials we go through that don't seem to have any purpose; they don't make sense. But one day, we will understand.

Not only will we see things more clearly, the Bible tells us that "God will wipe away every tear from their eyes; there shall be no more death, nor sorrow, nor crying. There shall be no more pain, for the former things have passed away" (Revelation 21:4). Think about that. It's hard to imagine a life without death, without sorrow, without crying, and without pain. But God has promised eternal life will be like that.

The next time you are feeling weary, sad, or distressed, remember that one day life will be better. Even if it's not better in this life, it will be better when we are living with God in eternity.

Going Deeper

1. Another person who is found in Hebrews 11 is Noah. Read Hebrews 11:7. How did Noah walk by faith?

Now turn back to Genesis 6:13-22. Why did Noah build the ark?

Noah's actions show us that he believed God. In two separate places it tells us that Noah did "all" that God had commanded him (Genesis 6:22; 7:5). It was by Noah's faith that he and his family were saved while everyone else was destroyed (Genesis 7:13, 23).

2. Before the Israelites were even placed in bondage in Egypt, God told Abraham that his descendants would "be strangers in a land that is not theirs, and will serve them, and they will afflict them four hundred years" (Genesis 15:13). Read

Genesis 15:14. What did God promise Abraham that He would do?

Now read Exodus 7-12. Did God judge the Egyptians as He had promised Abraham? Did the Israelites leave Egypt with great possessions? What did they leave with?

3. Have you been walking by faith with God? Examine yourself and journal about whether you have been trusting in God and the promises He has given us, or if you have been focused on the circumstances you are facing.

If you have been focused on your circumstances, talk to God about what is happening in your life. Tell Him how you've been feeling. Then cast your cares on Him. Remember that He cares about you and will be with you to get you through the trial.

AFTERWORD

EACH EBENEZER STONE IS A TESTIMONY. IT REPRESENTS SOME way that God has been faithful and shows how He has been working in your life. As we have seen, God is faithful to

- bring us into a relationship with Him;
- change us from the inside out so we are more like Jesus;
- provide for us, guide us, and protect us; and
- prepare us to do His work and then help us every step of the way.

God has also given us future promises that we can hold on to. We know that God will fulfill each one of those promises because He is faithful.

What Ebenezer stones have you seen in your life as you've read this book? Find a way to set up those stones as a memorial to what God has done in your life. You can use literal stones like I did or simply make a list.

For each stone, write out the way God was faithful and the date of the occurrence. The point is to have a visual reminder that you can look at to remember God's faithfulness. You can then use your Ebenezer stones to encourage yourself and others.

When you start to feel down or depressing thoughts slip into your mind, imitate the psalmist in Psalms 42 and 43. The psalmist

- poured out how he was feeling (Psalm 42:3-4);
- remembered how God loved him and gave him life (Psalm 42:6-8); and
- asked God to help him (Psalm 43:1, 3).

Then, the psalmist asked himself, "Why am I discouraged? Why is my heart so sad?" (Psalm 43:5 (NLT)). Finally, the psalmist made a decision to trust God. The psalmist told himself, "I will put my hope in God! I will praise Him again—my Savior and my God!" (Psalm 43:5 (NLT)).

Like the psalmist, you should pray to God about how you are feeling. Tell God what is going on in your life. Ask Him for help. Then get out your Ebenezer stones and remember what God has already done for you. Spend time thinking about the ways God has helped you. Make a decision to trust God. Praise God for His past faithfulness. Thank Him for His continued faithfulness. By faith, praise God for what He is going to do in your life in the future.

Share your Ebenezer Stones with others. Tell your family and friends about what God has done in your life. Let them know how God is currently working in your life. What has

God asked you to do and how is He helping you to accomplish it? Sharing these things will encourage you and those around you as you remember how God has been faithful. Praise God for what He has done. All the glory belongs to God because He is the One who helps us.

NOTES

Introduction

1. Olive Tree Bible Software, ed., *Olive Tree Enhanced Strong's Dictionary* (n.p.: Olive Tree, 2011), Strong's number g3049.

1. Remembering God's Faithfulness

1. Olive Tree, *Enhanced Strong's Dictionary*, h0072.
2. Olive Tree, *Enhanced Strong's Dictionary*, h0530.
3. Craig Groeschel, *Winning the War in Your Mind: Change Your Thinking, Change Your Life* (Grand Rapids, MI: Zondervan, 2021), 13.

2. Becoming a Child of God

1. Olive Tree, *Enhanced Strong's Dictionary*, h2398 (verb: hata), g0264 (verb: hamartano).
2. Leland Ryken, et al., "Sin," *Dictionary of Biblical Imagery* (Downers Grove, IL: InterVarsity Press, 1998).
3. Olive Tree, *Enhanced Strong's Dictionary*, h3091, g2424.
4. I put the church in quotation marks because the Mormons do not worship the same Jesus of the Bible, but that's an entirely different discussion.
5. Lee Strobel, *The Case for Christ: A Journalist's Personal Investigation of the Evidence for Jesus* (Grand Rapids, MI: Zondervan, 1998).

3. Growing in Spiritual Maturity

1. Lenya Heitzig, *Live Brilliantly: A Study in the Book of 1 John* (Colorado Springs, CO: David C. Cook, 2018), 86.
2. Olive Tree, *Enhanced Strong's Dictionary*, h3335.
3. Greg Laurie, "Still Thankful," *Pastor Greg's Daily Devo* (blog), November 25, 2020, https://harvest.org/resources/devotion/still-thankful/.
4. Olive Tree, *Enhanced Strong's Dictionary*, g5281.

5. Olive Tree, *Enhanced Strong's Dictionary*, g5046.
6. Jon Courson, *Courson's Application Commentary*, 3 vols. (Nashville, TN: Thomas Nelson, 2004), Olive Tree Bible Software, James 1:3-4.

4. The Good Shepherd

1. W. Phillip Keller, *A Shepherd Looks at Psalm 23* (Grand Rapids, MI: Zondervan, 1970), 61.
2. "Turkish Sheep Die in 'Mass Jump,'" *BBC News Europe*, July 8, 2005, http://news.bbc.co.uk/2/hi/europe/4665511.stm.
3. "Shearer Saves Lost Sheep From Woolly Death, Sets Unofficial World Record," *CNN*, September 4, 2015, https://www.cnn.com/2015/09/03/asia/sheep-record-wool-shearer.
4. "Baarack the Overgrown Australian Sheep Shorn of His 35kg Fleece," *Irish Times*, February 25, 2021, https://www.irishtimes.com/news/offbeat/baarack-the-overgrown-australian-sheep-shorn-of-his-35kg-fleece-1.4494836.
5. Courson, *Courson's Application Commentary*, Philippians 4:6.
6. Olive Tree, *Enhanced Strong's Dictionary*, h7993.
7. "Biography of George Muller," GeorgeMuller.org, accessed September 15, 2021, https://www.georgemuller.org/biography-of-george-muler.html.
8. Olive Tree, *Enhanced Strong's Dictionary*, g0574.
9. *It's a Wonderful Life*, directed by Frank Capra, featuring James Stewart, Donna Reed, and Lionel Barrymore (Los Angeles, CA: Liberty Films, 1946).
10. Olive Tree, *Enhanced Strong's Dictionary*, h3374.
11. Olive Tree, *Enhanced Strong's Dictionary*, g1167.
12. Olive Tree, *Enhanced Strong's Dictionary*, g4487.

5. Yielding to the Good Shepherd

1. Ed Taylor, "Thus Far the Lord Has Helped Us" (sermon), January 3, 2021, Calvary Church, https://calvaryco.church/view-all-messages?sapurl=LythZTVlL2xiL21pLys4d2g2ZzJ2P2VtYmVkPXRydWU=.

6. Doing God's Work

1. Olive Tree, *Enhanced Strong's Dictionary*, g3306.
2. Greg Laurie, "Not Ability, but Availability," *Pastor Greg's Daily Devo* (blog), June 1, 2012, https://harvest.org/resources/devotion/not-ability-but-availability/.
3. Olive Tree, *Enhanced Strong's Dictionary*, g5007.
4. Courson, *Courson's Application Commentary*, Matthew 25:14-30.

7. Walking by Faith with God

1. Olive Tree, *Enhanced Strong's Dictionary*, h3327.
2. *New World Encyclopedia*, s.v. "Sea of Galilee," accessed September 15, 2021, https://www.newworldencyclopedia.org/entry/Sea_of_Galilee.
3. Chayim B. Alevsky, "Dayenu: 'It would have been sufficient . . .,'" Chabad-Lubavitch Media Center, accessed September 15, 2021, https://www.chabad.org/multimedia/media_cdo/aid/255530/jewish/Dayenu.htm.
4. Olive Tree, *Enhanced Strong's Dictionary*, g1459.
5. Olive Tree, *Enhanced Strong's Dictionary*, g3956.
6. Olive Tree, *Enhanced Strong's Dictionary*, g2296.
7. Olive Tree, *Enhanced Strong's Dictionary*, g0166.

ACKNOWLEDGMENTS

FIRST AND FOREMOST, I AM GRATEFUL FOR GOD'S HELP IN writing this book. He is the One who created me, gave me the ability to write, and supplied everything I needed. It is only by His grace that I was able to complete it.

Next, I praise God for my husband. Matt has been so patient, encouraging, and supportive. He read each draft, provided insight and wisdom, ensured that I stayed on course, inspired me when I questioned my abilities, and gave me creative insight into design matters. I am thankful that Matt was there with me every step of the way as I wrote this book.

I would also like to express my deepest gratitude to all of the other people who helped make this book possible: my pastor, Ed Taylor, who has taught me much over the years by faithfully teaching through the Bible, chapter by chapter and verse by verse; Dawn, Jean, and Morgan, who provided feedback and encouragement; Micah Claycamp, who used his talents to design the book's cover; my friend, Jeana, who gave me a copy of Lee Strobel's book, *The Case for Christ*; and many others who have touched my life in various ways.

It has been a journey—an Ebenezer stone that I can set up to remember one more way that God has been faithful in my life.